China's Global Role

AN ANALYSIS OF PEKING'S
NATIONAL POWER CAPABILITIES
IN THE CONTEXT
OF AN EVOLVING INTERNATIONAL SYSTEM

John Franklin Copper

HOOVER INSTITUTION PRESS
Stanford University, Stanford, California

The Hoover Institution on War, Revolution and Peace, founded at
Stanford University in 1919 by the late President Herbert Hoover,
is an interdisciplinary research center for advanced study on
domestic and international affairs in the twentieth century. The views
expressed in its publications are entirely those of the authors
and do not necessarily reflect the views of the staff, officers,
or Board of Overseers of the Hoover Institution.

Hoover Institution Publication 226

© 1980 by the Board of Trustees of the
    Leland Stanford Junior University
All rights reserved
International Standard Book Number: 0−8179−7262−2
Library of Congress Catalog Card Number: 79−88585
Printed in the United States of America
Second printing, 1981
Designed by Elizabeth Gehman

To my wife

Contents

Tables

Preface

The onset of the 1970s saw U.S. President Richard Nixon announce a trip to China, the diplomatic recognition of the People's Republic of China by most of the nations of the world that did not already have diplomatic ties with Peking, and a vote in the United Nations to admit Mao's government to the world body—with a seat on the Security Council, a body reserved for the five major powers. Shortly afterward, the U.S. president went to Peking. Thus, in the course of a brief span of time, China became recognized as a legitimate member of the world community and a major actor in global affairs.

This process came to culmination at the close of 1978 with President Jimmy Carter's decision to grant diplomatic recognition to People's China on Peking's terms, and, in the eyes of many observers, to ally with China to offset the growing military power of the Soviet Union. Clearly, no other nation could serve this purpose. Alternatively, the U.S. move was seen to represent the reality that the world had become multipolar. In both contexts, observers made reference to China as the third or the new superpower.

These events represent a new situation, and role, for China. At the beginning of the modern era, it was weak and almost colonized by the West. Probably only an accident of history prevented colonization. The demise of Western imperialism brought several decades of internal strife and civil war to the Middle Kingdom. Subsequently, China sought to become an important member of the world community of nations but failed. In 1949, when the present regime came to power, Mao chose to align with the Communist bloc and limit China's intercourse with other nations. Efforts by the West, particularly the United States, and later actions by the Kremlin ensured that China would not break out of its isolationism and hence not play an important role in international politics.

Consequently, the decade of the seventies marks a change in China's participation in world affairs. It is also a time when the international system is evolving away from bipolarity to some other alignment. And the two events are not mutually exclusive or unrelated. The present thus may be described as a transitional period—for both China and the international community. It obviously contains some uncertainties. China's role in international politics is unclear. So is the future structure of international relations. This causes many observers to ponder China's new role—whether it will be a positive one or a negative one—and how it will affect the future international political system.

There already has been considerable speculation regarding China's strength and weakness. This has been done to anticipate the scope of its impact upon the international system and to determine where China will fit into the hierarchy of nations. Opinions vary. Some see China as a superpower; others argue that it is an underdeveloped country, too preoccupied with its own internal problems to alter the course of world politics or influence the global system.

This study constitutes an endeavor to measure China's national power capabilities, using time-tested measures of national power together with the most widely accepted quantitative data available on China. I hope to afford a more precise measurement of China's rank among the hierarchy of world powers by specifically assessing its ability to influence other nations and to play a role in world affairs. This will provide at least a partial answer to the problem of how to think and act toward China. The study will also facilitate our understanding of the current transitional nature of the international system. China undoubtedly will exercise some, perhaps considerable, influence on the development of a new style of international politics as we evolve away from the bipolar system.

However, trying to measure China's national power, either in the present or in the future, is difficult. China is not comparable to other nations in the ways usually used to measure national power. China possesses strengths that would put it in the category of superpower. Yet it is weak in ways that limit it to the status of minor power. Hence, the theories that have been developed to categorize nations or organize hierarchies of power do not apply well to China. They were created to compare the relative strengths of nations similar in size and level of development, in a conventional war. They also were designed to apply to a balance-of-power situation.

Nevertheless, no effort will be made here to develop a new theory of national power capabilities. Instead, I will synthesize several theories, typologies, and categories of elements of power already developed by other scholars. These will then be applied, with a great deal of flexibility and considerable interpretation, to this unique country, China, and to the specific question of its role in world affairs. Inasmuch as China must participate in the same global political arena as other nations, it is assumed that a formula or system that calculates national power in this context can apply, at least on relative terms, to China.

It is hoped that this work will add to our understanding of China's role in international politics as well as the influence of the international system on China. If the pages that follow help to provide a more accurate and realistic view of China's place in the world and make our accommodation with China easier, my purpose will be fulfilled.

1

Introduction: Views on China's Power Capabilities

The opinions on China's capacity to assume the role of a major power and exert a significant influence on international affairs span the gamut from extreme pessimism to ardent optimism and expectation. Both views are based on historical factors as well as on an assessment of China's national power capabilities. Unfortunately, because rapid change characterizes the present world, observations based upon historical lessons are not as useful as they might otherwise be. In any case, the advocates on one side pretty much balance those on the other and give us a divided or contradictory view. Similar difficulties arise when applying the concept of elements of power to China. In most assessments of China's power ranking, a few elements have been applied to the exclusion of other important ingredients of power, or they have been applied without consideration of the fact that China is not a developed Western nation and cannot be compared to other major international actors in this way. Moreover, due cognizance is not given to the fact that a nation's power, in either real or potential terms, must be seen in the context of an international system that is currently in the process of rapid change.

Inasmuch as China's rank among the world powers is both ambiguous and uncertain, it is essential to first assess two opposing approaches to the question of its power status—the historical, or subjective, approach and the power components, or objective view. Since there are now great expectations that China will play a major role in global affairs, greater attention will be given in this introduction to the arguments that it can and will become a great power. In subsequent chapters empirical data will be employed following the elements-of-power approach. This leads to a more pessimistic view of China's global role.

A study of Asian history evokes the view that China is a great nation. In East Asia, from prehistoric times to the modern period, China was the dominant, if not the exclusive, power. Moreover, it was the only permanent or lasting power. Mongols and other groups at times conquered much of Asia. They also controlled China, but could not ultimately subdue or control the Chinese, and even when they did China remained at the helm of Asian international relations. Thus most of the time through several millennia, interstate politics in Asia was a matter of the less civilized and weaker nations reporting to the Chinese capital and paying tribute. Furthermore, compared to the West, Chinese civilization was constant; it was not set back several centuries or eclipsed as was Western civilization when the Roman Empire was destroyed. And during various periods in world history, China was a nation of splendor, while the West languished.

The rise of the West and the fact that Western imperialism humbled China and exposed its inner weaknesses therefore can be taken as a temporary phenomenon. The view is also commonplace that China was weak, and the Western impact so great an embarrassment, because China was not ruled effectively—democracy never developed, political institutions were ineffective, and China's rulers were corrupt. Accordingly, many historians are led to the view that when these problems are resolved China again will become a powerful nation.[1] Amplifying this view, scholars of Chinese history also suggest that because of its humiliation China is now a "sleeping dragon" that, once disturbed, will trouble the whole world.

In 1949 the Communist victory over the Chinese mainland accentuated this view. Mao "captured" China and promised to make it strong again, and he made the West China's enemy. The pendulum of history, so to speak, was starting to swing back. Extending this perception, moral injustice had been committed against China and the West would have to pay for its transgressions. China would have to be accorded its deserved place in the world, and the accommodation would not be easy.

Several other modes of viewing China clearly bolstered the historical view of the inevitability of its rise to great power stature. First, China finally experienced the development of nationalism. This was a force that turned peoples into nations and nations into great powers. Mao's China was a nationalist one. Chinese leaders captivated the masses and taught them to love their country and to sacrifice for it.[2] China thus was united and became a nation in the real sense of the word. The energies of the Chinese masses could now be directed toward national reconstruction and toward another goal—that of making China a major world power.

Second, Mao's political system was described by Western scholars as totalitarian. This kind of rule, which had been seen only in Nazi Germany and Communist Russia, used thought control, mass regimentation, and police power to unify and direct the energies of the masses. According to the popular view, China had not only permanently resolved the problem of political fragmentation and ineffective rule but also had created a system that, for the purpose of becoming a world power, was superior to the political systems of Western countries.[3]

Third, Mao's rule was based upon a revolution that had application elsewhere in the world, especially in Asia, and could serve as an avenue by which China's newly found strength could be projected outwardly. Asia, for good reason, was thought to be fertile ground for communism, especially communism of a revolutionary sort. Thus it was assumed that Mao's Communist revolution could be transplanted to other countries in Asia and that communism as well as China's influence would spread.[4]

Underscoring the importance of these assets, China allied with the Soviet Union and became a prime mover in the international Communist movement. The West could do nothing to challenge China, since Mao had the Kremlin's nuclear protection. In terms of power, the two countries complemented each other, and in the eyes of independent observers the Communist bloc would grow: Soviet influence would expand in Europe and China's in Asia. Together they were a match for the West.

The first five years of Mao's rule in China also saw major accomplishments, particularly internally. The Chinese Communist party consolidated its rule and national reconstruction proceeded at a rapid pace. Productivity was quickly restored to former levels, and soon past records on almost all fronts were exceeded. After only five years it appeared that China would soon become a modern industrial state.[5] This, it was observed, would serve as the infrastructure for a powerful military machine—complemented by huge stores of manpower.

The Korean war simultaneously proved China's resolve and its military capabilities. It also made a clear imprint on the minds of Westerners—through human wave tactics, and an organized, well-trained, well-disciplined, and spirited army. This war was followed by conflicts elsewhere that continued to demonstrate Mao's courage and resolve: two offshore island crises, a war with India in 1962 that China won easily, and wars in

Vietnam, Laos, and Cambodia. Mao's statements to the effect that atomic bombs were paper tigers and that China could engage in a nuclear war, lose 300 million people, and still defeat the imperialists, also captured the attention of foreign nations and leaders. Thus, when China exploded its own atomic bomb in 1964, the world was even more convinced that China had become a great power and had to be recognized as such—lest the survival of mankind be endangered.

China's nuclear status evoked the view that the People's Republic must be admitted to the world community, even if on Peking's terms. Meanwhile, the Sino-Soviet dispute and the Vietnam war proved that China could weaken both superpowers and force change in the bipolar structure of the international system. China's differences with the Kremlin and Moscow's inability to force Mao to kneel to Soviet pressure gave rise to two kinds of communism, one Chinese, and split the world Communist movement. By the 1960s, when the rift between Moscow and Peking came into the open and proved genuinely serious, China had become a contending force in the Communist world while destroying the Soviet Union's leadership of the bloc and monolithic communism. In so doing, China significantly undermined the influence that one super-power could wield. The same thing occurred when, by fighting a war by proxy in Southeast Asia, China sullied the reputation of the United States as a global power and seriously weakened its national will. As a consequence of Vietnam, Washington foreswore its role as world police-man.[6] Thus, China dealt with the other superpower.

Simultaneously, while debilitating the two superpowers, China became recognized as a leader of various world revolutionary movements that promised to join forces and rally the poor nations against the rich. China therefore became a leader of the Third World—the poor, and the nonaligned majority. The result was that a world that was once two blocs led by the United States and the Soviet Union became three. The Third World, though not unified or organized, clearly became a third bloc. And if Peking could organize and lead these nations it might even force the Soviet bloc and the West into an alliance and give China control over an alliance of poor nations against the rich. Or at least so some perceived.[7]

In any case, China apparently accomplished what no other nation could—the destruction of the bipolar system. France had tried but did not succeed. No other nation had the strength or the will to engage in such a venture. Hence, the evolution away from bipolarity based upon a system dominated by Washington and Moscow was Peking's deed.

Whether the world was evolving toward a multipolar system, whether China would become a third superpower and a tripolar system would be the outcome, or whether the poor would be allied against the rich to constitute a new kind of bipolarity, China seemed destined to assume a role as a major world power.[8]

Some also perceived that the breakup of the old international system would give way to a universal system based upon internationalism and global equality. Should this system prevail, China's role would be a paramount one, since China accounts for more than one-fifth of the world's population. A system based upon an egalitarian perspective certainly would give China an advantage. This would be true both during the transition phase, during which time Peking could control a large bloc of human votes, and even later, since presumably China's votes plus those of its Third World allies would more than constitute a majority of the world's population.

The view that China is destined to become a major world power, if it is not already, is opposed by those who see no inevitability to history or little relevance in historical trends.[9] They point out that other historical powers—such as Egypt, Greece, Italy, and Turkey—are not likely to become world powers simply because they once were. Likewise, other nations were as mistreated by the West in the last century as China, and anti-Western nationalism is a widespread phenomenon in non-Western countries. The opponents of the view that China is or soon will be a major power also argue that China is still an underdeveloped nation and that its development plans have generally failed. They claim that continued unrest and turmoil within China reveal that it is not ruled effectively and that the respect and awe paid to China's unity and to the totalitarian model are unjustified. They also note that the Sino-Soviet dispute detracts from Peking's international influence and that China's leadership of the Third World is largely a figment of the imagination, since there is no such thing as a Third World bloc, and even if there were China would not be able to lead it. Following up this view, China is seen as still isolated and allied against, with no real friends in the world community.

Comparing the two views, it is clear that the optimistic view has been dominant in the last few years, although this was not the case in the 1960s. Such optimism is, in part, a product of the almost universal disappointment with the present bipolar international system and the style of international politics that it has produced. There is also considerable feeling that China has been wrongfully isolated by the West and by the bipolar system, and that this should and will change. Likewise, if there is going to be any move toward a universal system, whether this occurs quickly or in the distant future, China must be made a legitimate member of the international community and be given a voice in world affairs.

Having taken account of the historical, or subjective, approach, it is necessary to examine China's prospects of becoming a world power in terms of the concept of elements of power. First, some specific references to China's power or power potential will be made by assessing several views that certain elements of power are more basic or more important. Second, China's power potential will be appraised by using a list of ingredients of power. Again, high and low, or optimistic and pessimistic, estimates or judgments will be presented.

Several authors have isolated important or crucial elements of power in order to create a hierarchy of powers and have given China high marks. One scholar, for example, argues that national power is accurately reflected by an assessment of population and national income variables.[10] Thus, he gives China the potential to outrank all other nations in the world and predicts that this will, in fact, soon occur. Another writer considers population, iron ore, and coal reserves and suggests that China will "outgrow" the United States and the Soviet Union in the next century.[11] In still another study, wherein the researcher uses less specific components of power and defines a nation's power by its influence in conflict situations, China ranks third behind the United States and the Soviet Union but considerably above the fourth- and fifth-ranking nations, and is seen as the most rapidly growing power in the past two decades.[12]

The formulators of a national power equation that puts China in a less important position generally consider population as a contributory factor to national power only up to a certain point, at which time there are diminishing returns; or they give a prominent role to scientific and technological achievement.[13] One writer notes of China and India that they were not powers in the last century and will not be important national powers in the future because their population growth is uncontrollable and is a detriment to economic and scientific progress.[14] Those adhering to this view likewise generally agree with a point made by many students of nuclear age warfare that manpower has little or nothing to do with a nation's military capacity. Others who contend that China is not a major power and lacks such capacity, say that the future importance of nations is most directly related to their educational and economic capabilities—and here China ranks very low.

When a group of components or ingredients of national power is used, China also may appear either well endowed or weak. Although there is no agreement as to how many ingredients of national power there are (most lists vary from four to more than twenty), six categories will be used here, some of which are composed of more than a single element:[15]

1. Geography and population
2. Natural resources—which includes food and energy supplies
3. Economic strength—which encompasses industrial capacity and concedes to it a special place
4. Military power
5. Political system—including government control and stability, the will of the leaders, and the nation's diplomacy
6. Science and technology

These categories are synonymous with or include the most widely recognized ingredients of power and generally represent a fairly equal distribution of the important factors of a nation's global influence—although, as we will see in the final chapter, the weight of all of these categories will be affected by various trends and by the nature of the future international system.

An examination of the geography of nations shows that those lying in medium latitudes, which are large and possess natural borders, have an advantage over those that do not.[16] Location can be important in other ways; in fact, geopolitical advantages have long played an important part in the thinking of students of international politics.[17] However, there is no general agreement as to where the best location is. Large size is seen to be more important in the modern era, because small nations are especially vulnerable to nuclear attack and they generally lack within their borders sufficient population and resources. Population is considered equally important, since human resources afford the basis for a powerful army and a dynamic, growing economy. Numerous historical examples can be cited to show the advantage of a large population and high growth rates in enhancing national power status. Although some now say that this is no longer true, others still defend the need for a large and growing population, one that enjoys equality, freedom of travel, universal education, a free labor force, and other benefits. And it is generally agreed that world population controls only apply to the future.

A natural resource base in the broad sense includes food, energy, nonmetal and metallic minerals—all vital to the level of health and energy of the population, the development of industry, and the support of a modern army.[18] Additionally, resources can be sold to attain foreign exchange or investment funds for industrial development. Food is probably the most important natural resource, since it can be demonstrated that nations that have lost their food production capability decline proportionally in terms of their international influence. It is an obvious asset or weakness in wartime, while in peacetime it can provide a commodity that can be traded via exports for manufactured goods or technology if the country is still in a lower stage of development. A local supply of energy and metal and nonmetal resources is also considered a crucial advantage to industrial growth and competitiveness, and thus to national power status, especially in the event of economic warfare, embargoes, or sanctions. The impact of the Organization of Petroleum Exporting Countries (OPEC) on oil prices and the rising prices of other raw materials seem to indicate that this is a factor of growing importance in the global power equation.

The size and rate of growth of a nation's economy affect its power status inasmuch as a modern military system can be built and maintained only as a product of the industrial strength and the overall size and health of the national economy.[19] Historical as well as current examples can be cited as proof that this relationship was and remains valid. The United States and the Soviet Union are the world's largest economic powers and possess the largest, most advanced defense establishments. Thus they are called superpowers. Economic strength is also considered important for other, less vital but still important, reasons: it contributes to political stability and makes the population resistant to propaganda appeals; it increases a nation's trade and business ties with other countries; it is a stimulant to technological and scientific advancement.

Military power is the most apparent, and many say the ultimate, among national power ingredients.[20] Historically, military power was the only type of power measured. The most important considerations were the size of the nation's army, its weapons, training, and leadership. It can be argued that international politics is still based upon military strength and that the bipolar system, or whatever evolves from it, will reflect a world balance of military power. Defense budgets, flexible response capabilities, and intelligence are now more important in measuring a nation's military capacity, but the military factor remains crucial.

Effective government, political stability, the will to play a role as a world power, and an effective diplomacy are also important components of national power.[21] While these are frequently assumed to be specific assets, it is self-evident that the other elements of power cannot be made operational, or are less effective, if the nation's polity is weak. Certain systems are often accorded an advantage; for example, authoritarian systems are considered the most potent. The strength or resolve of the leadership of a nation and its capabilities in the area of diplomacy are also vital. The United Kingdom, for example, long enhanced its power status via an effective and stable political system and an astute diplomacy.

Although sometimes not accorded separate status, the level of development of science and technology is closely related to national power status. Most analysts now give science a much broader and more salient role, some giving it a paramount role vis-à-vis future world power status.[22] Certainly it seems to be the factor of power most likely to increase in importance in the future.

Using these elements of power as standards to measure China's capabilities, the optimist still espouses a sanguine view: China is particularly strong in categories 1 and 2—geography and population, and natural resources—and is generally advantaged in 3, 4, and 5—economic strength, military power, and a stable polity. Only in category 6—scientific development—is China handicapped, but based upon progress to date and the almost free flow of knowledge and technology, China will be able to catch up quickly.

A number of observers assert that in terms of geography and population in combination, China deserves the highest ranking of any nation in the world. This is also true of natural resources when iron ore, coal, and petroleum reserves are given high values. In neither area do the optimists see weaknesses that might handicap China. They generally give China comparable or slightly lesser ratings in economic strength, military power, and polity than the superpowers, but put China significantly above the other second-ranking powers; and they assert that China's potential in these areas is greater than all, or almost all, competitors. They either subsume science into a less important category or take the view presented earlier that, owing to China's progress in science and the fact that scientific knowledge is a free commodity, this is not a significant weakness for China.

The pessimistic view holds that in geography and population as well as in natural resources China is seriously handicapped or that it is not a significantly leading nation in either of these categories and will not be in the future. Those holding this view also argue that these factors are less important than some others. Regarding the other elements—economy, military, and polity—they do not give China high marks and see little hope for it to make a breakthrough or even major improvements in these areas. Or they see inherent weaknesses in all three of these ingredients of power that cannot be overcome. And they give greater weight to these elements and significantly more importance to science and technology than to categories 1 and 2.

Returning to the optimistic view, adherents of this standpoint tend to see the United States and the Soviet Union as relatively declining powers. And they argue that the other second-ranking powers all have significant weaknesses that make it impossible for them to compete with China for global status. France, Italy, the United Kingdom, and West Germany are mature and declining powers, weak in categories 1 and 2—geography and population, and natural resources. Japan is not so much a declining power as weak in areas 1, 2, 4, and possibly 5—geography and population, natural resources, military, and polity. India, Brazil, and some other large but undeveloped countries are behind China in all the elements of power. Two developed countries that otherwise may have considerable growth potential, Canada and Australia, are too seriously handicapped by their small populations to play an important role in international politics in the foreseeable future. Another part of this general view is that regional and other supernational organizations have not proved themselves viable and will not, at least to the degree that any of them will become an important international actor.

The pessimists, on the other hand, argue that the other second-ranking powers are not limited in any area any more seriously than China and that they will be able to overcome their weaknesses more easily than China. They give several important underdeveloped countries greater growth potential than China, and feel positive that Canada and Australia can attain important-nation status more quickly. And they see considerable promise in alliances and regional groupings of various sorts and other kinds of global actors such as multinational corporations, cartels, international organizations.

The six categories or ingredients of national power just cited provide the framework for an assessment in greater depth, in the following chapters, of China's specific strengths and weaknesses as they relate to world power status. Empirical and quantifiable data will be cited and comparisons made between China and the superpowers and other second-ranking powers. In the final chapter a broader assessment will be made, in the context of a global framework, of trends in the relative importance of each element of national power, and of the influence of the system's evolution away from bipolarity. Finally, the impact of the development of a new system upon the relative weight of each ingredient of power and China's specific strengths and weaknesses within each category will be analyzed. Since the majority view is optimistic but not well formulated, the conclusions generally appear pessimistic. This suggests that our expectations are too high. Indeed, the events of the early 1970s—the Sino-Soviet dispute and the Vietnam war—will not be repeated, and China will now have to compete directly with the superpowers for global status. In some respects China will play a major role in world affairs; in many, it will not. It is useful to know what these areas are and to prepare for China's entrance into the world arena.

The Geography and Population Factors

In terms of its physical size or land-surface area, China is the third largest nation in the world after the Soviet Union and Canada. It is slightly larger than the United States and somewhat bigger than Australia or Brazil. It is nearly three times as large as India and greater in size than any other nation by an even greater multiple (see Table 2–1). Compared to some other contending second-ranking powers, China is 18 times larger than France, 26 times larger than Japan, and nearly 40 times larger than Great Britain or West Germany.

Since large portions of the Soviet Union and Canada are frozen or barren, one could rank China at the top of the scale of the largest nations by land area with temperate climate. All of China falls within latitudes where the land can be used for agriculture and where temperatures are

TABLE 2–1

LEADING NATIONS BY GEOGRAPHIC SIZE
(square kilometers)

U.S.S.R.	22,402,200
Canada	9,976,139
China	9,596,961
U.S.A.	9,363,123
Brazil	8,511,965
Australia	7,686,848
India	3,287,590
Argentina	2,766,889
Sudan	2,505,813
Algeria	2,381,741
Zaire	2,345,509
Greenland	2,175,600

SOURCE: *United Nations Statistical Yearbook*, 1977.

conducive to the maximum use of human energy. In fact, China may be considered the largest nation in the world that is located in an area of ideal weather and temperature. Thus, in terms of size, China should be given a rank among the top three nations of the world along with the United States and the Soviet Union, and a ranking several places above any nation that will compete with it for world-power status.

China's margin of physical size clearly gives it an advantage over lesser nations that will compete with it for international influence. Its large size provides China with sufficient territory to make it a major producer of agricultural products and self-sufficient in foods, affords it large quantities of natural resources and makes possible the dispersion of industry and population so that a nuclear attack would not completely immobilize the nation, and makes a military invasion or occupation difficult. Clearly, the most serious contending second-ranking powers—France, India, Italy, Japan, the United Kingdom, and West Germany—lack these advantages. All but India, in fact, are seriously handicapped in terms of a bid to world-power status because of insufficient agricultural land. Italy, Japan, the United Kingdom, and West Germany are not self-sufficient in food, and all lack enough natural resources to maintain their industries. Unlike China, all of these nations are vulnerable to nuclear attack: an initial volley of nuclear blasts would render them impotent, with the possible exception of India. Finally, these countries are incapable of fighting a war of attrition, and they are vulnerable to sanctions or economic warfare as well as price increases or manipulations of a number of commodities on the world market.

Nevertheless, China's assets in this realm are not without qualification. Its large size does not afford it the advantages that, at first glance, seem apparent. Very little of China is too cold for agriculture but much of it is too high or too dry. Over one-half of China's territory is over one mile high.[1] In terms of quantity of arable land, China is far behind Australia, the Soviet Union, and the United States (see Table 2−2). Its advantage over India and several other nations is not as great as the land-surface figures suggest. In terms of arable land per capita, China is lower than any competing power except Japan. Moreover, China can increase the area of land under cultivation only slightly.[2] Finally, the land under cultivation in China does not contain a high percentage of good soil; the United States, with less total land area, has more than four times as much grade A land as China.[3]

Two other factors also come into play. China is overpopulated and,

TABLE 2–2

AGRICULTURAL LAND AREA IN BIGGEST NATIONS
(million square kilometers)

U.S.S.R	5,999.8
Australia	4,793.5
U.S.A.	4,413.0
China	2,873.5
India	1,770.6
Argentina	1,378.3
Brazil	1,267.3
Mexico	1,029.1

SOURCE: *Food and Agricultural Organization Yearbook*, 1965.

despite its large food-production capacity, actual production is barely sufficient to feed the nation. Although China exports a variety of food products, it also imports large quantities of grain, the amounts and costs of which have increased steadily over the last two decades. Moreover, the source of these imports is limited to a few grain-exporting countries, almost exclusively the United States, Canada and Australia. Thus, Peking is vulnerable to price increases, shortages, boycotts, and conceivably much more. These and related problems will be discussed in greater depth in chapter 3.

Because of its size, China is likely to have a greater variety and quantity of natural resources than most of its second-ranking power competitors. And this is the case. On the other hand, China is not well endowed in per capita terms, and lacks some important metal and nonmetal resources. This topic also will be discussed in chapter 3. Suffice it to say at this point that the important mineral assets that should accompany a large land area do not exist in China or must be qualified.

It is also questionable how advantageous China's size is in terms of allowing for the dispersion of population and industry so as to limit the effects of a nuclear attack. Ninety percent of China's population is concentrated on 15 percent of the land, which means that twenty to thirty nuclear blasts would annihilate a sizeable portion of the population.[4] The same is true of industry. In fact, the massing of industry into several industrial complexes has been a matter of concern for some time. In 1949, Mao attempted to decentralize industry to facilitate development in hinterland areas, but after 1957 this drive ceased. Thus, China's industry remains crowded into several relatively small industrial zones close to the coast.[5] Also, like other second-ranking powers that compete with China for world-power status, China's industrial centers are located near population centers. Thus, a limited nuclear attack by one of the superpowers, or an attack by a second-ranking power, would cause severe damage to both industry and population simultaneously. Rural areas in China might survive a limited nuclear war, but China's industrial strength or war-making capacity could not be restored immediately.

Obviously, China has an advantage in a conventional war over such countries as France, Japan, and West Germany—especially in a war of long duration. However, this advantage may not be as marked as it initially appears. As already noted, most of China's population and industry are concentrated, thus making it easy for a militarily superior enemy coming by sea to capture and hold much vital land area, as Japan did in World War II. Other areas are sparsely populated and house little industry or population. Cutting off pieces of China's sparsely inhabited territory would also be easy, especially for the Soviet Union, now China's most serious foe. A naval blockade, imposed by either superpower or even by some other strong naval power, would likewise be an effective military strategy against China, since much of the populated northeast relies upon the south or foreign imports for food, and land transportation is inadequate. Finally, because of low-quality medical facilities, germ, chemical, or radiological warfare would be very effective against China, in spite of the large amount of space.

Many of these points will be covered in greater depth in chapter 5, which deals with China's military capabilities. It is easy to see, however, that China's size is not the advantage that it was during World War II or that space might be for Australia, Canada, or the Soviet Union in dealing with a powerful adversary. Furthermore, it must be kept in mind that if either of the superpowers chose to make war against China, they would not need to invade China. Other second-ranking powers probably would not choose to do so; instead, they would employ strategic bombing or blockade, or would challenge China in other areas of the world. Thus, a war of attrition in which China might be a formidable adversary is unlikely.

China's geographic location or its geopolitical status, according to a number of observers, also provides it with an advantage over other nations. China is situated in the center, or on the hub, of the world's largest continent in terms of both physical size and population. In addition, much of Asia lies within the scope of China's historical influence. Today, many of the nations on China's periphery are small and weak and may well fall into the Chinese orbit. Thus, if China extends its influence beyond its borders, Peking will control much of the heartland of Asia. In contrast, the other powers are isolated, to a lesser or greater extent, from the mainstream of world activity by their locations. Certainly, no nation in the world has China's potential to gain such a sphere of influence by merely extending its influence beyond its border. This is particularly true of the second-ranking powers with which China will compete for power status. Japan and the United Kingdom are insular nations; France, Italy, and West Germany will have to compete with each other for influence in Europe; Australia and Canada are well removed from the mainstream of world activity; and India's influence is restricted to the South Asia subcontinent by the Himalayas and the Indian Ocean. Even the superpowers are isolated from the crucial areas of the world in a geopolitical sense.

On the other hand, such a sanguine view of China's favorable geopolitical situation can be challenged for a number of reasons. First of all, theories that uphold the critical or strategic importance of a specific land area have little or no foundation in reality. They were espoused by German and Japanese military leaders during World War II largely for ideological reasons, and were discredited by the course of war. They are certainly not popular now among serious scholars. A land-based geopolitical outlook was revived by the Kremlin after the war as a psychological means to bolster its power image, which at that time was substantially less than the West's. It also made communism appear to be the wave of the future in the sense that it could expand outward from a central land bastion.[6] Some strategists in the West, notably a number close to U.S. decision makers, accepted this reasoning, which led to the so-called "domino theory." However, time and events have not proved this view to be a sound one. Then, for the theory to apply, China and the Soviet Union must be allies; today, this is far from the case.

In any case, competing with the Communist land-based geopolitical view are theories that emphasize sea zones and air lanes. These other theories do not place China in a crucial location; in fact, China is clearly in a disadvantageous position, according to alternative geopolitical theories. A number of writers argue that because of new weapons of war, the United States and the Soviet Union are blessed in terms of location as far as international influence is concerned, since they do not need to keep their military at home to defend their borders; instead, they can utilize it as an arm of their diplomacy and global influence.[7] This is particularly true of the United States. The same advantage may be said to accrue to Australia and, to a lesser extent, to Canada, India, Japan, and the United Kingdom. It obviously does not apply to China.

China's geography also presents some obvious handicaps. China is disadvantaged by having few natural frontiers. Its only natural boundary is the mountain barrier between southwest China and India, and here the border was drawn to favor India in terms of strategic passes and transportation links. China's other borders are not natural and most were delineated by Western colonial powers to China's disadvantage.[8] In Southeast Asia, the terrain favors China's opponents in the event of either a conventional war or guerrilla conflict. Coupled with this liability, most of China's border provinces are populated by minority groups whose loyalty to Peking is questionable. Southwest China is populated by Tibetans who are hostile to both communism and Chinese. In western China, there are a number of tribes of European origin that wish to maintain their autonomy and thus are willing to collaborate with the Soviet Union. Over the past decades, many of them have fled across the border. They now constitute a potential guerrilla force if Moscow wants to arm them and send them back to China. In northern and northeast China, Mongols and Manchurians make up a sizable portion of the population and their attitudes toward Peking are subject to speculation.[9]

The fact that China has a long, unnatural, and difficult-to-defend frontier, which on China's side is populated by minority groups, means that Peking must keep large numbers of troops in border areas. This precludes a concentration of military forces in one area to deal with a single adversary, and it means that a large Chinese army must be maintained simply to provide for the country's defense. In fact, China has more nations on its border, more insecure frontiers, and more controversies with neighboring states than any other large or small power (see map, p. 18).

China's border with the Soviet Union is a subject that deserves special mention. This 4,150-mile-long boundary is longer than the border between any other two countries, is unnatural, and is not even demarked in places. Moscow has fortified the border with over 44 divisions plus modern weapons of various kinds, including nuclear weapons. In addition, China's 2,700-mile-long border with Outer Mongolia, which is a Soviet satellite, adds to the dimension of the problem. This border is dangerously close to China's capital and its industrial heartland. Soviet missiles and armored divisions are positioned on this border only 400 miles from

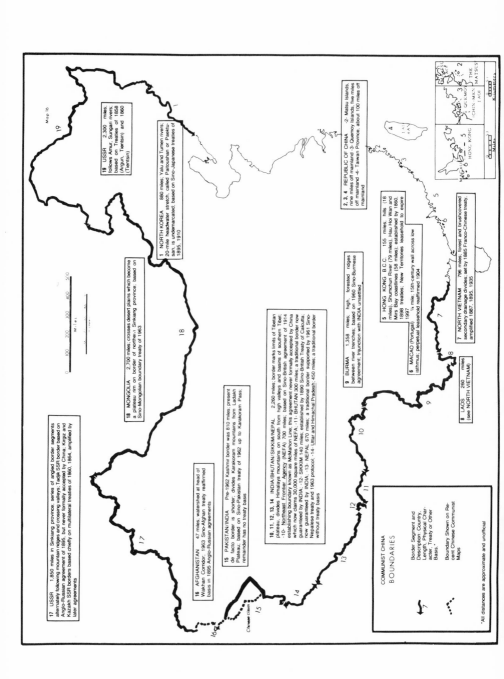

Peking. China keeps a large portion of its military forces on its northern borders—yet it is still outgunned. And, China is vulnerable here at all levels of warfare—nuclear, conventional, guerrilla. The proximity of enemy troops and weapons, in addition to the serious danger of either direct or indirect military conflict, means that Chinese military forces can be constantly put on alert or tormented by activities on the border. China cannot respond in kind, since the Soviet Union is militarily stronger and its capital and population center are far from the border. Certainly, no other nation in the world is disadvantaged in this way—having a long, unnatural border with a hostile superpower.

Another problem that may be defined as geopolitical is that of unresolved territorial claims. China lays claim to more territory within the boundaries of other nations and has more outstanding disputes with other nations over unsettled boundaries than any nation on earth. Moreover, the referents of its territorial claims include both superpowers and the other two major powers in Asia—India and Japan—as well as Great Britain (see Table 2−3). These claims are a serious impediment to China's diplomacy with the involved nations, not to mention the fact that several territorial claims have created crisis situations in the past. China's opponents use these claims to document Peking's aggressive foreign policy and its irredentist designs. In those cases in which China claims territory in dispute with Vietnam and the Philippines, Peking is made to appear an imperialist power, thus sullying its reputation among Third World nations.

TABLE 2−3

CHINA'S TERRITORIAL DISPUTES WITH OTHER NATIONS

Nation	Disputed Area
U.S.S.R	Sino-Soviet border
Japan	North China Sea, Senkaku Islands
Korea	North China Sea
U.K.	Hong Kong
Portugal	Macao
China	Taiwan, Pescadore Islands, Quemoy and Matsu, Senkaku Islands, South China Sea
U.S.A.	Same as above via alleged U.S. aid to Nationalist China
Vietnam	South China Sea and islands
Philippines	South China Sea and islands
India	Sino-Indian border

SOURCE: A. Doak Barnett, *Uncertain Passage: China's Transition to the Post-Mao Era.* (Washington, D.C.: The Brookings Institute, 1974).

In population, China easily ranks first in the world, considerably above the superpowers and many times larger than any other second-ranking power except India (see Table 2−4). China's population exceeds that of the Soviet Union and the United States by multiples of four and five, respectively. Compared to France, the United Kingdom, and West Germany, China's advantage is twentyfold; compared to Australia and Canada it is forty times or more. And based upon current birth and death rates, the gap between China and its second-ranking competitors is widening. Consequently, China's edge in population size undoubtedly will remain in the foreseeable future.

China's huge population is a contributing factor to its national power status for a number of reasons. Most arguable is that it will help guarantee China's survival as an important power in the event of a nuclear war. If Peking engages one of the superpowers in a limited nuclear exchange, or even a second-ranking power in a full atomic-scale war, it will have a distinct advantage. For example, if China and France or the United Kingdom (or Japan, if it becomes a nuclear power) engage in a nuclear exchange—assuming an equal number of hits—China will certainly emerge the victor. The advantage of a large population is even more marked in conventional warfare, which, considering that nuclear weapons have not been used in the post-World War II era, seems more likely. Large population size makes high casualty figures tolerable. Also, human resources remain available to sustain large military operations and provide manpower for reconstruction.

TABLE 2−4

LEADING NATIONS BY POPULATION* IN 1976

China	852,133,000
India	610,077,000
U.S.S.R.	256,674,000
U.S.A.	215,118,000
Indonesia	139,616,000
Japan	112,768,000
Brazil	109,181,000
Bangladesh	80,558,000
Nigeria	64,750,000
W. Germany	61,513,000
Italy	56,169,000
U.K.	55,928,000
France	52,915,000

SOURCE: *United Nations Statistical Yearbook,* 1977.
*Figures are for mid-1975.

In addition, based on its huge manpower resources, China's standing army compares with those of the two superpowers and dwarfs the other second-ranking powers. China's regular military is now larger in size than U.S. forces and is only slightly smaller than the Soviet Union's. Compared to other second-ranking powers, China's advantage is severalfold. And this is only China's standing military force. Counting its reserves, militia, and other groups with military training, China's armed forces are many times larger—almost equal to the total population of the Soviet Union or the United States. Obviously, in the event of an ordinary war, China would be a formidable opponent. For this reason, it is often maintained in military circles that it would be suicide for any nation to engage China in a conventional conflict or try to invade China. In addition to its direct use in combat, China's large army also gives Peking a potent instrument of coercion over other Asian nations, particularly those on or close to China's border. It is for this reason that many analysts believe that China will ultimately dominate Asia.

China's immense population is seen as an asset for still other reasons. In economic terms it gives Peking a huge labor force, which as economic growth proceeds, may guarantee increasing economic productivity. A large population can also be advantageous in providing a large market for the mass production of goods. As the United States has demonstrated, this is a tremendous advantage in competing with other modern, but smaller, industrial countries. Presumably, China will be able to take advantage of this market as it modernizes and as industry turns to consumer products. A vast population also supplies a large human resource base for scientists and other highly skilled people, and since geniuses tend to make up a small but consistent percentage of the population China is advantaged. Presumably, as China's educational and technological infrastructure grows, Chinese leaders will be able to make fuller use of its "brain reservoir" and this will greatly facilitate scientific achievement and technological progress.

A number of trends in world politics also may favor nations that have large populations. Probably most important is the growing emphasis on equality—which will give large nations increased voting power in international organizations. There is likewise evidence that population size will soon be taken into consideration in allocating welfare and other benefits of global organizations. And travel and emigration restrictions probably will be lowered in future years to the advantage of nations that are overpopulated. Thus, nations that can export people can also export influence. If international standards are set for population control, those nations with currently large populations will probably be advantaged in terms of future national power.

The aforementioned points, however, must be seen against certain countertrends and the clear liabilities that a large population presents, which may outweigh the advantages. Certainly the ledger sheet contains both a credit and a debit side.

The contention that a large population, especially in an underdeveloped country, is an advantage in nuclear warfare is no doubt true. But it has no application vis-à-vis the superpowers, since they are in possession of arsenals that can destroy even small centers of population or cause pollution by the use of atomic weapons such that few, if any, could escape the residual effects. Thus, China's population size would mean little or nothing in an atomic war with the Soviet Union or the United States. Also, rural areas in China would be affected in a total conflict with a second-ranking power if that power employed germs, chemicals, or radiological weapons. The advantage in such a situation could well be with a more developed country, even though smaller, that could take precautionary or defensive measures, rather than with a country that is large and essentially rural. This is notably true of germ warfare—probably the strategic weapon with the greatest potential after nuclear weapons.

China's advantage in a conventional war is axiomatic; yet, one must consider the probability of a conventional war between China and any other second-ranking power. Lacking logistical capabilities, China's military manpower has almost no application to any second-ranking power, with the exception of India, and even here the mountainous area separating the two countries would severely limit the magnitude of any conventional war in that area and thus the importance of manpower. Peking would have an edge in a conventional war against the Soviet Union, assuming the Kremlin did not escalate the conflict by using larger weapons. But there is no reason to believe that such a limit has any meaning. Certainly the Soviets have given no cause to believe that it would. In fact, Soviet military leaders base their military strategy vis-à-vis China upon superior fire power and a rapid escalation to larger weapons, including nuclear weapons. China's manpower advantage over the smaller Asian countries on its border or near it is more meaningful, but the limitation here is that most of these nations are allied with one of the superpowers and have some guarantees from them that probably would prove operational in the event of a Chinese invasion or even the threat of one.

Although conventional war seems more likely in the future than nuclear war, guerrilla war and interventionism are even more probable. In the latter two types of conflict, military manpower has little relevance. In guerrilla campaigns, only small forces can operate effectively without being detected; intervention requires sophisticated intelligence, transport, and logistics capabilities rather than a large army.

The argument that a large population affords an equivalent labor force, which in turn guarantees economic growth, also must be qualified in the Chinese case. First, while China's labor force is large, because of the young age of the population, it is not as large a percent of the population as that of most competing countries. Over 40 percent of the population is under age 15 and 60 percent is under age 25.[10] In addition, because of the lack of mechanization in the agricultural sector, two-thirds of China's labor force is tied to the farms and communes.[11] Second, only a small portion of the labor force is skilled. Hence, it has been argued that China does not have significant quantities of usable labor for rapid industrial development. Meanwhile, the excess of unskilled labor impedes the use of labor-saving devices and thus tends to brake technological progress.[12]

Related to the argument that a large population guarantees a large labor force is the theory, also gained from Western economic development experience, which asserts that a growing population ensures a dynamic economy and thus economic progress, because it guarantees a growing market and fosters innovation. The Western model, however, assumes a small population base in relation to land and investment, which is clearly not the case in China. It also assumes the expanding use of technology. Likewise, the advantage of scales of production based upon a large marketplace clearly does not apply to China at its present stage of development for two additional reasons: an inadequate transportation system makes China essentially a fragmented economy or a conglomerate of small economic units, and consumer goods are not produced in China in large quantities. Therefore, it is questionable whether the Western experience, which suggests definite advantages of a large and growing population vis-à-vis economic development, has any validity for the Chinese situation. Then, one must consider the counterargument: that a large and growing population (that is, an overpopulation problem) is a drain on investment resources and hence slows economic growth in compounding terms. The calculation that a 1 percent increase in population in crowded, underdeveloped countries absorbs 10 to 12 percent of national income seems to be more relevant to China.[13]

The thesis that a nation's power status is improved by the ability to draw on a large human-resource base to produce scientists, engineers, and technicians similarly appears to have little relevance to China. The argument that a big population automatically produces a large number of good engineers, scientists, and technicians is belied by the importance of a high investment of capital per capita in scientific training. Although this point will be discussed at greater length in chapter 7, it should be noted at this juncture that U.S. scientists are trained at costs varying upward from $100,000, and their work is sustained with comparable expenditures. Furthermore, even in the richest countries, there is far from a full utilization of scientific talent due to the high costs of research.

For the reasons just mentioned, among others, most scholars of China's demography agree that China's optimum population is probably considerably less than it is now, and certainly less than that of the Soviet Union or the United States. Chinese leaders already seem aware of this and are endeavoring to reduce the birth rate. If population control in China becomes successful, as present trends indicate it will, China's international influence based on population size will diminish. At the present time, although China's population growth exceeds that of the superpowers and the other second-ranking powers, except India, it is well below the world's average.[14] Nearly every country in Latin America, Africa, and Asia is experiencing more rapid population growth than China (in the Far East, for example, only Japan and Singapore are lower). Thus from the 1960s to the end of the century, based on present trends, China's share of the world's population will drop from one-fourth to one-fifth. And, if the present trends are projected, India will be larger in population than China in less than four decades.[15] Consequently, those who argue that population growth is a positive factor influencing national power must admit that China is gaining only versus certain competitors; it is not gaining versus India or the rest of the world in general (see Table 2-5).

Finally, international trends toward equality are unclear. Human rights and self-determination are obviously becoming a part of world culture; but so too are national sovereignty and the equality of nations. The two sets are in contradiction, and it is uncertain which will prevail. Probably the latter will for several decades. And although international emigration has increased somewhat in recent years, it is not as commonplace as it was several decades ago and probably will not be for some time to come—maybe only after the world population problem is resolved.

TABLE 2–5

POPULATION GROWTH OF SELECTED COUNTRIES AND REGIONS, 1965–1973
(births per thousand population, per year)

Latin America	2.89
Africa	2.67
Oceania	1.95
World's average	2.02
India	2.10
China	1.70

SOURCE: United Nations, *World Statistics in Brief*, (New York, 1976).

Certainly there is no move at present to allow overpopulated nations emigration rights to less-populated regions.

China's huge and growing population has also been the source of some problems not yet mentioned. For example, it fosters fear in other nations and has had a negative effect upon Peking's diplomacy. All of the nations on China's periphery have expressed some apprehension of China's expansionist desires in the context of its overpopulation problem.[16] Some of them used to welcome Chinese immigration; none of them do now. In fact, several nations in Southeast Asia have forced Chinese residents to return to China and others have allowed or encouraged discrimination and even the killing of Chinese. Peking has tried to make it appear that birth control efforts are a plot of the rich and imperialist countries, in its appeals to the Third World, but this has clearly failed. In short, inconsistent policies and proclamations on the question of population control have done little but sully China's credibility and image abroad.[17]

Up to this point only the standard means of measuring physical size and population have been cited. If some other methods of calculation are used, China may not appear so large in either category and, again, the trends do not appear to be favorable. One way of assessing a nation's physical size is to measure the amount of land within its borders, together with the size of its allies. Another approach might consider other actors besides nations, such as various kinds of regional organizations or alliance systems, as competitors for international influence. Still another is to count space that nations control, both land and sea areas. The same may be done in measuring population size.

If China is compared in physical size to a number of regional economic or alliance systems, there are at least ten that are larger than China. Below is a list of some of them, ranging from OPEC, which is slightly larger, to the British Commonwealth, which is three times the size of China (see Table 2−6). Some, if not all of these, are important actors in international politics, and they will certainly compete with China for global status and influence. It is important to note in this connection that China is not a member of any regional system, alliance (except the Sino-Soviet alliance that is now considered void), or cartel. And there is no reason to believe that this situation will change in the near future.

A similar way to view territorial size in order to assess national power status as it applies to global influence is to look at trade ties, movements of people and labor, language commonalities, and so forth, that link certain nations into partnerships or groups. Using such criteria, the United States and Canada could certainly be seen as a single actor and are so viewed by the Soviet Union and China. The English-speaking nations may also be seen as global partners, as are the members of the European Economic Community. Large segments of Latin America and Africa may become so some day. In contrast, China has little potential of uniting with any other country in Asia—even North Korea and Vietnam—or any existing regional organization, to increase its size.

Still another way to measure territorial size is to consider claimed or jurisdictional territory, territorial waters, and the control of land or sea areas. Territorial claims to or control of areas in outer space likewise may be considered. Land surface claimed by the United States and Australia in Antarctica, if added to their national territory, would make both of these nations larger than China, not to mention territory under the jurisdiction of both. Great Britain and France also have considerable "juris-

TABLE 2−6

TERRITORIAL SIZE OF LEADING TREATY ORGANIZATIONS AND BLOCS
(square kilometers)

British Commonwealth	28,190,418
Organization of African Unity	26,337,093
COMECON	24,955,224
Warsaw Pact	23,392,366
NATO	22,228,969
ANZUS	17,336,647
Latin American Free Trade Association	16,099,875
Organization of American States	15,055,875
Arab League	13,613,174
OPEC	9,983,182

SOURCE: *United Nations Statistical Yearbook, 1977.*

dictional" territory. China has no such "adjunct" territory. Similarly, a number of nations increase their size appreciably by counting claimed ocean space as part of their national territory. Since its coastline is significantly smaller than that of other nations of similar size and because it shares its territorial sea with several other nations, China is much less able to increase its size in this way than most other large countries.[18] And since the United States and the Soviet Union have made the first and only important ventures into outer space, their territory might be perceived to have increased proportionally. Thus, territorial claims, no matter how they are viewed, reduce China's relative size and its rank by physical size in the hierarchy of large nations.

Similar arguments may be made concerning China's population size, although to a somewhat lesser extent. If regional and economic blocs and military alliances that are considered major world actors are compared to China in terms of population, China's advantage is lessened considerably. The population of the British Commonwealth exceeds China's, and a number of other global actors are close to China in population size (see Table 2−7). Moreover, several of these blocs are experiencing population growth rates that exceed China's.

In conclusion, it appears that China has some advantage over most of its second-ranking competitors—France, India, Japan, the United Kingdom, and West Germany—in terms of its size and population. It does not have an advantage over the Soviet Union or the United States in real size, especially when U.S. jurisdictional territory or territorial areas are added, or if Canada is included as part of the United States, which, for economic

TABLE 2−7

Population of Leading Treaty Organizations and Blocs, 1976
(thousands)

British Commonwealth	954,755
North Atlantic Treaty Organization	565,619
Organization of American States	540,737
COMECON	384,826
Warsaw Pact	370,065
Organization of African Unity	366,068
OPEC	273,674
Association of Southeast Asian Nations	233,342
Latin American Free Trade Association	192,703
Arab League	147,249

Source: *United Nations Statistical Yearbook*, 1977.

and defense purposes at least, it should be. China has a significant edge over both the superpowers and all of the second-ranking powers except India in both population size and in population growth. But at this juncture, past judgments of national strength based upon a large and increasing population do not seem to be very relevant. Clearly, the liabilities of a large population that is growing too fast are considerable. Consequently, although China has an edge over Australia and Canada because of their small populations, and over the short run this probably will remain true, its larger population cannot be seen to give China an advantage vis-à-vis the United States or the Soviet Union. It may accord it some advantage over most other second-ranking powers, but hardly a significant one. In a conflict, China's huge population cannot be seen as an asset, save in a border conflict or conventional war on or near China's soil. It does not have direct application to a direct engagement between China and any other second-ranking power, and, with the possible exception of a conflict with India, it is hard to see in what situation China's population is advantageous in military terms vis-à-vis a competing power. China's geopolitical situation is also questionable. It seems to be favorable only if past geopolitical theories are accepted and if China can become a superpower. Finally, when territorial and population comparisons are made and applied to global influence, which the term *power* is here intended to mean, it is necessary to consider various military alliances and economic, language, cultural, and other ties. When this is done, China's rank is reduced considerably.

3

China's Natural Resource Base

In terms of its resources, here defined to include agricultural land, metal and nonmetal elements, and fuels, China appears to have tremendous potential—approaching, if not equivalent or even superior to that of the superpowers. However, there are certain impediments or limits to the use of its resources to attain greater power status. In fact, how big an asset China's resources are is subject to considerable speculation. In the past, China was widely thought to be resources-poor; now that this is recognized to be untrue, some exaggeration has supplanted the earlier view. Clearly, a more careful analysis is needed in the context of China's efforts to become a major world power.

As we have already seen, China's agricultural land is vast, although not as plentiful as its overall size would suggest, due to the fact that a considerable amount of China's surface area is high in elevation or is dry. On the other hand, nearly all of China lies within favorable climatic zones. And at least some of the areas where elevation or lack of water now present a problem can become usable in the future. In the important agricultural areas, the topsoil is thick and has been cared for well, though most of the soil is not as rich as in the best agricultural areas of the U.S. and many other countries.

China's agricultural assets, together with the skills and tenaciousness of its farmers, make it one of the leading agricultural nations in the world—second only to the United States in total food production. In rice output, China leads the world. In most other important grains, it ranks near the top and well above competing second-ranking powers (see Table 3–1). China is the world's foremost producer of pork and ranks high in the raising of other meat animals (see Table 3–2). In basic food production, China outranks most of the nations of similar power status,

TABLE 3-1

LEADING WORLD GRAIN PRODUCERS, 1976
(thousand metric tons)

	Rice		Wheat		Barley		Oats		Corn
China	129,054	U.S.S.R.	96,900	U.S.S.R.	69,539	U.S.S.R.	18,113	U.S.A.	159,173
India	64,373	U.S.A.	58,307	China	15,401	U.S.A.	7,930	China	33,114
Indonesia	23,000	China	43,001	Canada	10,513	Canada	4,831	Brazil	17,845
Bangladesh	17,627	India	28,846	France	8,319	Poland	2,695	Romania	11,583
Thailand	15,800	Canada	23,587	U.S.A	8,111	W. Germany	2,497	U.S.S.R	10,138
Japan	15,292	Turkey	16,587	U.K.	7,648	China	1,900	Yugoslavia	9,106
Vietnam	10,800	France	16,150	W. Germany	6,487	Finland	1,573	S. Africa	7,312
Brazil	9,560	Australia	11,713	Spain	5,473	France	1,402	Mexico	8,393
Burma	9,307	Italy	9,516	Turkey	4,900	Sweden	1,251	Argentina	5,544
S. Korea	7,243	Pakistan	8,691	Denmark	4,801	Australia	1,072	France	5,851

SOURCE: *United Nations Statistical Yearbook,* 1977.

TABLE 3–2

LEADING WORLD FARM ANIMAL PRODUCERS, 1976

Pigs		Cattle		Sheep	
(million head)				(thousand head)	
China	238.3	India	180.3	Australia	148.6
U.S.S.R.	57.9	U.S.A.	127.9	U.S.S.R.	141.4
U.S.A.	49.6	U.S.S.R.	111.0	China	74.5
Brazil	35.5	Brazil	95.0	New Zealand	56.4
W. Germany	19.8	China	64.6	Turkey	41.4
Poland	18.8	Argentina	58.2	India	40.2
Mexico	12.1	Australia	33.4	Argentina	35.0
France	12.0	Mexico	28.7	Iran	35.3
E. Germany	11.5	Bangladesh	28.0	S. Africa	31.0
Romania	8.6	Ethiopia	25.9	U.K.	28.3

SOURCE: *United Nations Statistical Yearbook,* 1977.

and challenges the superpowers. In other agricultural commodities, China is similarly productive: tobacco, first in the world; tea, second; potatoes, third; and sugar, sixth.[1]

Based on its high productivity, China is a traditional exporter of a number of agricultural commodities such as rice, soybeans, sugar, cotton, dried and canned fruits, and vegetable oils. This generally remains true today. In 1974, China exported 2 million tons of rice, which, at the market price of $400 per ton, earned $800 million in foreign exchange.[2] Its canned and dried fruits can be found in marketplaces throughout the world. By-products from agriculture also constitute an important part of China's export sales. Although China has had food deficits in the past, there have been no serious shortages in recent years; and calorie and protein intake, on the average, are sufficient. The reason for this is the increasing productivity of agriculture. In the last decade, China's overall agricultural production has increased by 30 to 40 percent.[3] Improvements in farming techniques, more irrigation and fertilizer, and new seeds are having considerable impact, and promise to give China even better harvests in the future.

On the other hand, there are severe limits to increasing agricultural production in China, and a breakthrough in food production cannot be expected. China's agricultural land area appears to be barely sufficient to feed its large population and may be inadequate given future population increases. China is slightly larger than the United States, yet it has 35 percent less arable land and four to five times as many people to feed. In terms of usable agricultural land per capita, China is very low on the scale of nations—0.34 hectares per capita compared to 1.9 in the United States. Here China ranks even lower than India.[4] The amount of arable land per farm worker is even lower, making increases in yields much more difficult to achieve than in most countries.[5] And there is little prospect of opening up new lands to farming; most estimates are around 2 to 3 percent. In fact, in 1958, with more intensive farming methods put into operation, the amount of land under cultivation decreased. It increased in subsequent years, but there has been no gain since 1973. In recent years, on the average, more farmland has been lost to industry than has been added by opening up new lands, and the amount of land under cultivation in China now approximates and may even be lower than the figure for the mid-1950s.[6]

In the last ten years, more fertilizer has been used in China, which accounts for better yields. In fact, the use of chemical nutrients increased more than ten times in the seven years prior to 1974 during which time China became the world's largest importer of chemical fertilizer.[7] Irrigation has increased almost proportionally. Double cropping has also increased and the use of miracle seeds has contributed to much higher yields. All of these methods continue to hold some promise, but a breakthrough, if this term is appropriate, has undoubtedly already been made. Future increases will be slower, since China has already absorbed most of the present know-how in these three areas.[8] Some progress can be anticipated from large water-control projects, but this will be at considerable capital expense. More efficient utilization of manpower, incentives, more investment in agriculture, and better planning also seem to offer avenues of improvement; but again, limits will be realized quite quickly.

A brief survey of agricultural policy in China will further help to elucidate the obstacles to significantly increasing productivity. Since the Communist regime came to power in 1949, various methods have been tried to increase agricultural production. In the early years it was land redistribution and rural cooperatives. In the late 1950s Mao sought to absorb rural disguised unemployment by instituting a new revolutionary agricultural system that would merge the agricultural and industrial sectors via the communes. To his dismay, he discovered that there was not the amount of idleness in the rural sector that he had thought, and that it could not be put to work in the industrial sector. Nor could industry be merged with agriculture to increase efficiency and productivity.[9] In the wake of the failure of the Great Leap Forward, the government invested more in agriculture and, according to its own figures, up to 1971 spent 23.4 percent more on agriculture than it received back in taxes from the agricultural sector of the economy.[10] This situation remains. Recent programs that focus on increased irrigation and fertilizer use have stepped up production, but at considerable financial investment. Clearly, future increases in agricultural productivity in China depend upon even more investment in the agricultural sector. But if China is to continue its efforts to industrialize, it cannot afford to divert more capital for agriculture. Demonstrating this fact, in 1974 imports of fertilizer were cut back due to a balance-of-payments problem.

Thus, China's agricultural sector may be regarded as about as productive as it can be. It may be able to keep up with continued population growth, but even this is uncertain. Clearly, it will not serve as a major source of needed investment capital. Global comparisons based upon potential agricultural growth suggest that it is highly unlikely that China will increase its agricultural productivity as fast as the rest of the under-developed world, where there is considerable land that can be put under cultivation and where the use of fertilizer, irrigation, and better seeds has only begun to improve yields.[11] Those nations of the underdeveloped world that manage to hold down their population growth rates will undoubtedly become food exporters in the future. In the meantime, Australia, Canada, New Zealand, the United States, and a few other nations possess the "food weapon," which, in recent years, has become quite a potent force in international politics.

The magnitude of China's food exports is also deceptive. In the past, China exported certain food commodities, including rice, but did so largely because of inadequate internal transportation facilities and because it had little else to sell that had a market abroad. It exported rice from the south while it imported other grains in the north. After 1949 the government increased both exports and imports because the price of rice was higher than the other grains China imports.[12] This situation generally remains, although it is uncertain how long the price gap between rice and wheat will last. Because China trades extensively in agricultural products, and because of the regime's policy of publishing only favorable statistics, it appears that China is a major exporter of agricultural commodities. Indeed, China is a major seller of rice. But this is the only grain that it sells, and although it sells more rice than other countries, rice does not constitute a large portion of the world grain trade as do wheat or corn. A look at world export figures shows that China is not a large exporter of grain when compared to the United States, Canada, and Australia (see Table 3–3).

China's rice exports must also be seen against its imports of other grains.[13] The amounts and values of the latter have increased steadily and have risen faster than China's rice exports (see Table 3–4). Meanwhile, some other agricultural commodities that China traditionally exported, such as soybeans, cotton, and sugar, are now imported. Finally, because the sources of its imports are limited, China is vulnerable. It imports large stores of grain from the United States, Canada, and Australia (see Table 3–5). These three nations could easily form a cartel

TABLE 3–3

LEADING NATIONS BY GRAIN EXPORTS, 1976
(thousand metric tons)

Wheat		Rice		Corn	
U.S.A.	26,537	China	2,190	U.S.A.	44,295
Canada	10,553	U.S.A.	2,107	Argentina	3,080
Australia	7,567	Thailand	1,869	Netherlands	2,476
France	7,336	Pakistan	782	Thailand	2,355
Argentina	3,155	Burma	600	France	2,046

SOURCE: *Food and Agricultural Organization Yearbook* (Rome, 1976).

TABLE 3–4

CHINA'S GRAIN IMPORTS

Year	Amount (million metric tons)	Value (million U.S. dollars rounded to nearest $5 million)
1961	6.2	435
1962	5.3	370
1963	5.7	400
1964	6.8	475
1965	5.7	400
1966	5.6	400
1967	4.1	295
1968	4.4	305
1969	3.9	260
1970	4.6	280
1971	3.0	205
1972	4.8	345
1973	7.7	840
1974	7.0	1,145

SOURCES: A. H. Usack and R. E. Batsavage, "The International Trade of the People's Republic of China," in *People's Republic of China: An Economic Assessment; People's Republic of China: International Trade Handbook* (Washington, D.C.: Central Intelligence Agency, September 1974).

TABLE 3–5

(million metric tons)

	Wheat	Corn	Total
U.S.A.	2.01	0.77	2.78
Canada	1.90	—	1.90
Australia	1.39	—	1.39
Argentina	0.14	0.59	0.73
France	0.21	—	0.21

Source: Arthur G. Ashbrook, Jr., "China: Economic Overview, 1975," in *China: A Reassessment of the Economy* (Washington, D.C.: Joint Economic Committee of the U.S. Congress, 1975).

to force the price of grain upward, or withhold it for political reasons. Although this does not appear to be an immediate danger, China is dependent upon these countries in a way that affects its flexibility in global politics.

From the point of view of international influence and power status, China's agricultural resources are not contributory and there is little hope that this will change. In fact China is vulnerable because of its food imports which it cannot offset completely by its agricultural exports. Although the United Kingdom and West Germany are also vulnerable because of needed food imports, they have resolved this problem, or at least have reduced its significance, by membership in the Common Market. India and Japan, nations that are similarly food importers, have a higher priority with the food-exporting countries than China. The United States, Canada, and Australia enhance their global influence with food exports and doubtless will continue to do so in the future. For these three nations and, to a lesser extent Argentina and France, the food weapon is a significant asset in world politics. If one speculates regarding other nations that may acquire the food weapon, it would be the underdeveloped, underpopulated countries. They certainly have much more potential to produce food surpluses than China. The same is probably true of the Soviet Union even though, in recent years, it has had deficiencies in agricultural production.

In conclusion, China can be thought of as rich in agricultural land and large food production, but not in per capita terms or in any way that will make it a major power other than by supporting its already large population. The agricultural sector will not likely serve as the stimulus of rapid industrial growth as it has in many other countries. Nor is China in pos-

session of food power, as are the United States and several second-ranking powers such as Canada and Australia. Finally, future increases in
food production are uncertain. Expectations range from slight surpluses
in the future to severe shortages. The former would allow China at least
moderate industrial growth and a considerable amount of economic self-
reliance; the latter would hurt China's development and could make it
dependent upon several traditional Western enemy nations.

China possesses sufficient, if not plentiful, quantities of most metal
and nonmetal resources. It has the world's largest reserves of some, such
as antimony and tungsten. Where a number of others are concerned, it
ranks among the world's top nations in terms of potential extraction (see
Table 3–6). At present, most of China's natural resources have not been
fully exploited, so there is considerable promise for gains in the future in
mining and resource extraction, as well as in production and sales. There
is little doubt that both in quantity and variety China's storehouse of
natural resources compares to the two superpowers and ranks it far ahead
of any second-ranking power.

In calculating the importance of China's resources relative to the
world-power game, there are three respects in which China's favorable
endowment of resources may give Peking an edge in the world-power
competition. First, China's resources will guarantee its continued industrial development based upon indigenous sources of raw materials at
constant prices. In short, industrial progress in China will not be affected
by price increases of raw materials in the world market. Rather, China
will be protected from rising prices as well as shortages. Second, China
will be immune to economic warfare or boycott. Third, China can use the
sale of its resources for profits and thus investment capital. Finally, China
may provide free supplies to assist its allies or force neutral countries to
take sides with it on global or regional political issues. In view of rising
prices and possible scarcities of a large number of metal and nonmetal
resources, this may prove to be a powerful tool of diplomacy and a means
of considerable external influence.

Most of the other countries with whom China will compete for power
status are not as blessed in terms of natural resources as China. Several—
France, Italy, Japan, the United Kingdom, and West Germany—are re-
source-poor and are vulnerable to fluctuating prices and availability, not
to mention boycotts and blockades. Australia, Canada, and India are better off, but do not have the wide range or the quantity of resources that
China possesses. The two superpowers appear to have greater quantities

TABLE 3-6

CHINA'S METAL AND NONMETAL RESOURCES

Commodity	Approximate Rank in World Output	Share of Estimated World Output (percent)	Adequacy in Production	Reserves or Resources
Metals				
Aluminum	9	2%	Virtually adequate	Considerable
Antimony	1	24	Large surplus	World's largest
Bismuth	5	7	Large surplus	First rank
Chromite	Insignificant	Very small	Greatly deficient	Unimportant
Copper	10	2	Deficient	Moderate
Gold	Not among first 20	Small	Can use more	Moderate
Iron ore	4	6	Adequate	First rank
Iron, pig	5	6	Adequate	Not applicable
Iron, steel ingot	7	3	Adequate	Not applicable
Lead	9	4	Slight surplus	Moderate
Manganese ore	6	6	Surplus	Considerable
Mercury	4	9	Large surplus	First rank
Molybdenum	5	3	Sizable surplus	First rank
Nickel	Insignificant	Very small	Greatly deficient	Unimportant
Tin	2	13	Large surplus	First rank
Tungsten concentrate	1	30	Large surplus	World's largest
Zinc	11	3	Slight surplus	Moderate
Nonmetals				
Asbestos	5	4	Moderate surplus	Considerable
Barite	8	3	Slight surplus	Considerable
Cement	8	3	Slight surplus	Extensive raw materials
Fluorspar	5	8	Sizable surplus	Considerable
Graphite	5	7	Adequate	Moderate
Gypsum	13	1	Adequate	Considerable
Magnesite	3	11	Surplus	First rank
Phosphate rock	7	1	Seriously deficient	Considerable
Pyrite	5	6	Can use more	Considerable
Salt	2	13	Slight surplus	First rank
Sulphur	8	2	Surplus	Moderate
Talc	5	4	Surplus	Moderate

SOURCE: *Mineral Review Yearbook of the Mineral Industry of Mainland China* (Pittsburgh: U.S. Department of Interiors, 1975).

of most resources than China, but their stocks of many resources are being rapidly depleted or are already used up. Thus, China may be seen to have an advantage even vis-à-vis the United States and the Soviet Union in this realm.

However, this view must be balanced by a more detailed analysis of China's resource assets. An appraisal of potential discoveries and exploitation in the rest of the world and an up-to-date assessment of the relationship between resources and national power is necessary.

Figures on the amount and quality of China's natural resources are still estimates and, to some extent, are based on speculation. Due to the fact that China's resource base was grossly underestimated in the past, recent estimates tend to be off on the plus side. Moreover, for purposes of enhancing its image as a world power, Peking has encouraged over-estimates and has released some surveys that have been grossly inflated. Thus, when production figures are compared to resource estimates, a gap is instantly perceivable (see Table 3–7). A lag in production, of course, explains part of this gap, which stems from the fact that China's mining capabilities are still backward, as are its finishing facilities. In any case, both of these factors—the overestimating of China's resources and its problems in resource exploitation—tend to reduce China's strength in this area in terms of world influence.

An examination of world production figures on various metals over a period of two or three decades reveals that China's ranking among world producers is not improving. This is the result of a faster rate of resource

TABLE 3–7

CURRENT STATUS OF CHINA'S PRODUCTION OF SELECTED METALS

Aluminum	Sizable quantities imported from Australia, Canada, France, and Japan
Antimony	Sizable exports to Japan and the United States
Bismuth	Production steady at 250 tons annually; no exports
Copper	Demand exceeds domestic production by two to three times; imports from Chile and Zambia
Iron	Production increasing slowly; imported 3 million tons in 1973, chiefly from Japan but also from the United States and West Germany
Lead	Steady production at 100,000 tons; world rank in production has dropped
Zinc	Steady production at 100,000 tons; world rank in production has dropped
Manganese	Steady production at 1 million tons; world rank in production has dropped
Mercury	Remains major world producer, but no significant exports
Tin	1.5 to 2.0 millions tons held in reserve; exports up, especially to Japan and the United States
Titanium	Production sufficient for domestic needs
Tungsten	Production and exports increasing

SOURCE: *Mineral Review Yearbook of the Mineral Industry of Mainland China* (Pittsburgh: U.S. Department of Interior, 1975).

discovery in other areas of the world, in addition to improved extraction techniques used elsewhere. Technologies in both areas are available to many of the underdeveloped nations through joint-venture agreements with the industrial countries, to the advantage of both. China's unwillingness to engage in such agreements for political reasons accounts, in part, for the fact that production has not kept up with discovery in China. China's inadequate transportation system is also a factor. Resources in a number of areas of China cannot be utilized economically due to inaccessibility.

Again looking at production figures, it is evident that China is not a leading producer of any of the most important metals, except for iron—where its ranking in world production is fourth, and manganese—where its rank is eighth (see Table 3–8). Likewise, China does not possess abundant quantities (that is, sufficient for significant export) of any of the critical metals used in weapons production or high-technology industry. Antimony, tungsten, and tin—the metals in greatest abundance in China—are considered neither important nor critical metals.[14] Finally, China is not in possession of large quantities of any metal that is subject to cartelization. In fact, several years ago Peking sought to control upward the world price of antimony, mercury, and wolfram by withholding sales for a number of months, but this had little or no effect on the market and the efforts were discontinued.[15] Contrariwise, China lacks sufficient quantities of several metals that are essential in manufacturing (copper, aluminum, nickel, and chromite are the most important) and that are potentially subject to cartelization.[16] This is particularly true of copper, which China imports in large quantities. Peking's present sources of copper are Zambia and Chile, countries that are regarded as politically unstable.[17] China also imports platinum, ruthenium, iridium, and industrial diamonds.[18]

Iron, the most important metal in the industrial process, is found in vast quantities in China, but it is generally of low quality and the location of mines is not favorable for either domestic use or export. For this reason, China's steel industry has grown very slowly in recent years, and China imports scrap iron as well as finished steel. Steel imports currently amount to more than 10 percent of China's use and come chiefly from Japan.[19] This is balanced by Japan's imports of Chinese oil, and it probably could be compensated by imports from other countries such as West Germany and the United States in the event China's relations with Tokyo change. However, this could still be a potential problem, considering the

TABLE 3–8

Leading Producers of Most Important Metals*

(thousand metric tons)

Iron		Aluminum		Manganese		Zinc		Copper		Lead	
U.S.S.R.	105,374	U.S.A.	4,902.9	U.S.S.R.	2,847.5	Japan	776.0	U.S.A.	2,077.1	U.S.A.	1,259.2
Japan	88,584	U.S.S.R.	1,600.0	S. Africa	1,895.0	U.S.S.R.	720.0	U.S.S.R.	1,460.0	U.S.S.R.	500.0
U.S.A.	78,804	Japan	1,450.7	Brazil	1,141.5	U.S.A.	651.9	Japan	922.5	W. Germany	349.1
W. Germany	32,088	W. Germany	697.1	Gabon	1,091.0	W. Germany	473.7	Zambia	694.6	Japan	267.8
China	30,000	Canada	628.1	Australia	770.6	Canada	472.3	Chile	632.0	U.K.	251.4
France	19,519	Norway	618.8	India	549.7	France	251.5	W. Germany	607.0	Australia	199.8
U.K.	14,024	U.K.	540.2	Ghana	313.0	Belgium	241.2	Canada	534.3	Canada	175.7
Italy	11,888	France	518.4	China	300.0	Poland	236.7	Zaire	274.0	France	172.2
Canada	10,026	Italy	404.5	Mexico	145.1	Australia	204.5	Poland	270.1	Mexico	163.2
India	9,996	Netherlands	255.5	Morocco	140.9	Italy	201.7	Australia	176.7	Belgium	121.5

SOURCE: *United Nations Statistical Yearbook*, 1977.

*Figures are for 1976, except manganese, which is for 1974.

amount that comes from Japan and the fact that China's other sources are, almost exclusively, Western countries.

In total metal production, generally regarded as more important than resource reserves when measuring national strength, China is not among the top ten nations of the world. And for a variety of reasons it is unlikely that this will change very much despite the existence of large untapped ore deposits in China. First, China is not rich in resources on a per capita basis. Only in the production of tungsten concentrate is China above the world average. In all other metals China is below average, and in most considerably below, when a per capita calculation is used. Second, resource production requires considerable investment in mining and production facilities as well as a continually improving technology. Both investment funds and technology are scarce in China. Third, for ideological reasons China is unwilling to sign agreements with foreign companies to export either raw ores or finished metals so as to improve its mining and production capabilities. Even if Peking were to change its position in this regard, it would not have much immediate effect in view of its own industrialization plans. In contrast, all of the nations with whom China will compete for national power rank, except India, are major producers of the most important metals as well as a wide range of nonmetal resources. Reflecting their special status, the superpowers rank at the top in the production of the important metals and near or at the top in the less important metals and nonmetal resources.

Although many of the advanced countries have exhausted or are in the process of using up their domestic supplies of raw materials, this does not necessarily put China in a relatively favorable position when considering future trends. Various metal and nonmetal elements can now be extracted from the sea by mining the seabed or by the distillation of seawater. Two of China's plentiful metals, iron and manganese, hold the most promise for sea mining. Mercury, which is also plentiful in China, can be obtained from seawater. Resource substitution is also increasing. Two other metals plentiful in China, tin and tungsten, can be replaced by aluminum and molybdenum, respectively. Finally, most of the metals in wide use in the United States and other Western nations are now being recycled.

The fact that cartels have not been successful (except perhaps in the case of uranium) and that the prices of most raw materials have fallen after a marked rise after 1973 and are now lower in real terms than twenty to thirty years ago, suggests that indigenous sources of raw materials may not be as crucial to a nation's power status as we are often led to believe and as was the case in the past.[20] Certainly, countries like Japan, that do not have natural resources, have experienced no serious problems. In fact, Japan's record to date seems to be living proof of the declining importance of native sources of metal and nonmetal resources. The expanding world market in resources and increasing use of technology in locating and extracting natural resources may ensure that this will remain true in the future. If, however, it turns out that the reverse is true, the Soviet Union, Australia, Canada, and the underpopulated, less-developed countries that can export raw materials without sacrificing their own industrial growth or standard of living will benefit most.

In summary, China is protected from economic boycott, cartelization, and scarcity to a considerable extent by its adequate sources of most metal and nonmetal resources. Industrial planning and growth in China is also favored by assured sources of raw materials at constant prices. Finally, considering its small amount of trade, China is fortunate to have local sources of raw materials. However, until China improves its backward transportation system, it will have difficulty using its resources adequately. Also, because of lower costs of sea transport, China's own sources of raw materials are not an advantage in terms of cost-efficiency over importing countries like Japan. China will no doubt continue to sell some resources, thus providing a source of foreign exchange; but current trends indicate that such sales will continue to decline in amount, relative value, and importance.[21] Meanwhile, China is increasing its importation of several resources, especially metals, at a rapid rate.[22] Clearly, the sale of resources will not constitute a means whereby China can satisfy a serious need for capital, nor will it give Peking membership in or control of a cartel or even influence over the price or flow of any important resources. In the future, it may only offset China's purchases.

China's energy resources have been the basis of even rosier predictions concerning its future world power status, and compared to China's food, metal and nonmetal resources, the prognostications are indeed better. China is blessed with large coal, petroleum, and natural gas deposits, vast hydroelectric power potential, and apparently significant quantities of uranium and other radioactive elements. Estimates of its coal reserves rank China from first to third place in the world.[23] China's oil and natural gas deposits put it among the top ten nations in the world, while some estimates of its petroleum reserves put China above even Saudi Arabia and considerably above the United States or the Soviet Union. China's water power potential is judged to be equally high, estimated at between 540 and 580 million kilowatt hours if fully harnessed.[24] No reports have been published on China's uranium deposits, but it is assumed that they are also significant, at least judging from China's nuclear weapons progress, which has relied solely upon domestic sources of uranium and plutonium.

Currently, China is the world's fourth largest producer of energy after the two superpowers (see Table 3–9). It is the world's fourth largest consumer of energy after the United States, the Soviet Union, and Japan.[25] If energy production and consumption are accurate reflections of national power, and many political analysts argue that they are valid barometers, China clearly is a power of the first order. No other second-ranking power comes close to matching China's energy production, and only Japan (which imports nearly all of its energy) is in the same league as far as consumption is concerned.

Since a modern nation depends upon energy, and the world's supplies have diminished while prices have multiplied, a plentiful supply of energy now seems crucial to national power status. The actions of the OPEC cartel in 1973 and after clearly demonstrate the vulnerability of most of the second-ranking powers that compete with China for world influence. France, Japan, the United Kingdom, and West Germany were shown to possess a serious weakness in energy self-sufficiency. This was also true of India and many countries of the underdeveloped world. It was even true of Australia and the United States. After the crisis passed, the developed Western countries experienced rapid inflation combined with economic slowdown or depression. This has led some analysts to question

TABLE 3–9

LEADING NATIONS IN ENERGY PRODUCTION, 1977
(equivalent of thousand barrels per day of oil)

U.S.A.	29,678
U.S.S.R.	24,315
Saudi Arabia	9,543
China	8,237
Iran	6,139
Canada	4,774
U.K.	3,330
Poland	2,496
West Germany	2,321
Kuwait	2,125

SOURCE: *Handbook of Economic Statistics* (Washington, D.C.: Central Intelligence Agency, 1978).

whether or not nations with no energy resources of their own can engineer rapid economic growth in the future.

During the energy crisis, China continued to experience rapid industrial growth and was almost untouched by inflation. Its energy production increased by around 9 percent a year, led by annual jumps of 20 percent in petroleum production.[26] After 1973, China became an important exporter of oil—a tremendous boon in terms of foreign exchange. With this profit, Peking purchased machinery and technology abroad to further its ambitious industrial development plans and bought fertilizer plants to facilitate agricultural production and weapons to bolster China's defense capabilities.

The political impact of China's oil sales has also been considerable. By selling oil to Japan, Peking apparently kept Tokyo from concluding a deal with the Soviet Union to develop oil and natural gas deposits in Siberia, which would facilitate the Soviet Union's economic development as well as improve its military capabilities on the Sino-Soviet border. In short, it helped preserve a diplomatic distance between Tokyo and Moscow that otherwise might have been bridged. Oil deals also helped maintain China's influence in North Korea, and have facilitated establishing diplomatic ties on favorable terms with a number of other Asian countries, most notably Thailand and the Philippines. It may even have had some influence on the U.S. China policy.

Looking at the other side of the coin, China's biggest energy asset, in terms of known reserves, is its vast coal deposits, which, as already stated, compare to or exceed those of the United States and the Soviet Union, placing China in either first, second, or third place in the world in reserves. China's coal, however, is chiefly bituminous coal, which is high in pollution-producing elements. Moreover, most of China's coal reserves are both inconveniently located and difficult to mine. Already, the best mines have been worked out. This explains why the domestic demands for anthracite and coke have not been met and why shortages have been reported in recent years. In the past decade, the growth in China's coal production, overall, has been less than 4 percent annually, while there has been no increase since 1973.[27]

This situation has led some experts to reappraise China's coal resources in terms of immediately recoverable or useful deposits. When this is done, China does not compare favorably with the United States or the Soviet Union and, in fact, is outranked by Western Europe in total reserves (see Table 3–10). There may be technological breakthroughs in

TABLE 3-10

LEADING NATIONS AND REGIONS IN RECOVERABLE COAL RESERVES
(megatons)

U.S.A.	181,781
U.S.S.R.	136,600
Western Europe	126,775
China	80,000

SOURCE: *Survey of Energy Resources* (Washington, D.C.: Central Intelligence Agency, 1974).

the near future which will bring to market China's coal that cannot now be utilized; but new mining technology will no doubt help the superpowers more, especially the United States, as well as the Western European powers such as France, Italy, the United Kingdom, and West Germany, since they have to overcome energy deficits. Even if China could mine more coal, its industrial development would benefit only marginally because of the already widespread conversion to oil. Foreign sales would increase, but due to inadequate transport facilities, in addition to the high pollution content of Chinese coal, one should not anticipate sales abroad on any large scale. Finally, it is fairly certain that environmental problems will soon affect China as they have the United States and other industrial countries. Two problems in this area particularly affect China: air pollution and strip mining. The former is already evident in China's big cities; the latter ruins farmland—a problem more serious in China than in other countries, due to the shortage of arable acreage. Both of these problems can be surmounted, but not without considerable difficulty and investment. Thus, China's coal must be regarded as a secondary or reserve energy asset at the present time.

Similar problems will hold back China's development of hydroelectric power. China's potential here is considerable, although careful scrutiny reveals that Peking has published highly optimistic estimates. Thus, its water power potential should be described as moderately high but not fantastic. Then, there are obvious obstacles. The biggest impediment to the further development of this resource is the fact that the most easily harnessed water power lies in south and southwest China—the least industrialized and least populated areas of the country. To utilize electricity produced from dams built in these areas would necessitate long transmission lines or moving industry into these areas. There is less, but still considerable, hydroelectric potential in north and central China. But here, a major problem is silting and the danger of ruining large expanses of agricultural land with damming. In addition, dams in these areas would be expensive and risky undertakings for a number of other reasons, among them the frequent occurrence of earthquakes. It is because of these problems that China has not increased by much its hydroelectric power in the last two decades.[28]

China's most impressive advances in recent years have been in the exploitation of its petroleum reserves. But current evidence justifies only moderate optimism. First of all, initial production increases do not necessarily mean that such gains can be maintained over a long period of time. In fact, the 20 percent yearly increases in oil production for 1973–1975 dropped to 15 percent in 1976 and 8 percent in 1977.[29] Thus, China's rapid expansion in this area seems to be slowing, and it appears reasonable to predict annual increases in the range of 10 percent or less in the next decade. Many of the easily exploited deposits have been tapped and some have already dried up. To continue to increase production at a rapid rate China will have to drill deeper wells and work offshore, which will require more capital and technology—both in short supply.

There are also a number of other obstacles to increasing China's oil production and sales. At present the country's largest oil fields are in the north, but not adjacent to the coast or close to major seaports or industrial centers. Thus, there is a problem of transport to both domestic and foreign markets. Also, the climate is inhibiting in these areas. Added to this, Chinese petroleum produces about 70 percent heavy oil, which is not as marketable as lighter oil, and is heavy in paraffin content, which makes refining more difficult. Some underdeveloped countries, in fact, have experienced problems using Chinese oil.[30] There are also political impediments to increasing oil production for sale abroad, as violent protest demonstrations in 1976 point out.

Currently, China is selling sizable quantities of oil to Japan, and this serves as an important source of revenue. Chinese petroleum, however, constitutes less than 5 percent of Japan's total imports, making it impossible for China to use oil sales as a means to pressure Japan politically. Japan, moreover, is hesitant to increase its purchases from China and will probably resist raising by much the relative size of its Chinese supply. Meanwhile, Japan is still exploring the possibility of a joint oil exploitation agreement with the Soviet Union. Tokyo has also made significant investments in oil production in Indonesia and several Middle Eastern countries. Another factor to consider is the speculation that the southern part of Japan is sitting on one of the largest oil deposits in the world. China will probably seek alternative markets, but the significant ones are the United States and Western Europe. In both cases, distance and other problems present formidable barriers.

Finally, it is uncertain whether or not oil prices will continue to escalate. The OPEC cartel may weaken.[31] Some members want to increase oil production; others want to reduce the supply. Some want to increase the price; others do not. In any case, China is not a member of OPEC and has made no serious efforts to join the organization. Saudi Arabia, with whom China does not have amicable relations, appears able to control the future price of oil, thus eliminating the possibility of Peking gaining even an indirect influence on international oil prices or sales. It is even possible that China will come to loggerheads with OPEC because it sells at below cartel prices. China's entrance into the United States or Western European markets will certainly increase the risks of a confrontation.

China's capacity to increase its oil exports must also be juxtaposed with its own requirements relative to its industrialization plans. China's recent annual expansion rate in energy production has been in the 9 percent range. For China to sustain a growth rate of 6 percent in gross national product, considering the present relative needs of the agricultural, industrial, and service sectors of the economy, will require an 8.5 percent annual increase in energy production simply to meet domestic demand.[32] This does not leave much surplus for export. Clearly, Peking's projected 50 million tons annual export to Japan after 1980 cannot be realized easily. In fact, Peking probably will have to scale down its industrial growth and cut back fertilizer production, upon which increasing agricultural production depends, if it is to export the quantities of oil it says it will—unless, of course, there are unforeseen breakthroughs in production.

China's current oil production gives it a rank of tenth in the world (see Table 3–11). Since its reserves rank it in almost the same position—in fact, in a lower position—it is unlikely that China will increase its relative rank very quickly, if at all (see Table 3–12). This suggests that it is improbable that Peking will improve its world position as an oil exporter. Looking at its prospects in still another way, even if China sustains its annual increases in oil production at 18 percent, which is above current increases and therefore hardly likely, it will export in 1985 only 10 percent of OPEC's 1974 exports. This does not give Peking a great deal of international influence based upon oil power.

China's natural gas production also puts China in a top rank among

TABLE 3–11

LEADING NATIONS BY OIL PRODUCTION, 1977
(thousand barrels)

U.S.S.R.	10,700
Saudi Arabia	9,200
U.S.A.	8,200
Iran	5,660
Iraq	2,330
Venezuela	2,240
Nigeria	2,100
Libya	2,080
Kuwait	1,970
China	1,806
Indonesia	1,690
Abu Dhabi	1,660
Canada	1,320
Algeria	1,040

SOURCE: *Handbook of Economic Statistics* (Washington, D.C.: Central Intelligence Agency, 1978).
*Includes shale oil and small quantities of synthetic oil.

TABLE 3–12

LEADING NATIONS BY KNOWN OIL RESERVES, 1977
(million barrels)

Saudi Arabia	150
Kuwait	67
Iran	62
U.S.S.R.	35
Iraq	34
Abu Dhabi	31
U.S.A.	30
Mexico	30
Libya	25
European Community	20+
China	20
Nigeria	19
Venezuela	14
Indonesia	10
Canada	8
Algeria	7

SOURCE: *Handbook of Economic Statistics* (Washington, D.C.: Central Intelligence Agency, 1978).
*This includes offshore oil claimed by several European countries; therefore, Western Europe is entered as a bloc rather than by separate nations.

the nations of the world (see Table 3–13). However, its reserves are slightly less, in relative terms, than its production (China ranks fourteenth in the world in reserves) and its exports to date have not been large.[33] The same problems hamper China's sales of natural gas as limit its petroleum exports.[34] China's uranium deposits are apparently sufficient to build atomic bombs, but there is no evidence that its uranium or other

TABLE 3–13

LEADING NATIONS IN NATURAL GAS PRODUCTION, 1977
(thousand barrels per day oil equivalent)

U.S.A.	9,701
U.S.S.R.	5,740
Canada	1,562
Netherlands	1,521
China	872
U.K.	662
Romania	661
Iran	393
West Germany	301
Italy	236

SOURCE: *Handbook of Economic Statistics* (Washington, D.C.: Central Intelligence Agency, 1978).

radioactive elements are plentiful or can serve as the basis of developing atomic energy for generating large quantities of electricity. World estimates of nations' uranium deposits do not even list China.[35]

In making an overall appraisal of China's energy capabilities, particularly to give it a ranking among world powers, it should be noted that while China's energy production gives it a relatively high world-power rank, it is still less than one-third of the Soviet Union's output and one-fourth that of the United States. Furthermore, China's energy production is not far ahead of a number of other nations that are not considered competitors for world-power status, such as Canada, Iran, and Venezuela. When China's energy production is compared to various blocs which in this realm are obvious international actors, its rank diminishes even further (see Table 3–14). China's energy production capabilities seem to be somewhat larger than its current production, but its domestic requirements will increase with further industrialization, probably keeping pace

TABLE 3–14

KNOWN OIL RESERVES BY BLOC OR CARTEL

	Amount (billion barrels)	Percent of World
OPEC	427	77.8%
Arab OPEC	382	69.6
Soviet bloc	36	6.5
NATO	66	12.0
China	20	3.6

SOURCE: *Handbook of Economic Statistics* (Washington, C.D.: Central Intelligence Agency, 1978).

with increases in production. Measuring reserves instead of production, China has a higher ranking (that is, closes the gap) in comparison to the superpowers and most other second-ranking powers. But compared to blocs rather than to individual nations, the conclusions are quite different. China's reserves are small compared to those of the United States and its allies, the Soviet bloc, or OPEC.

China's energy resources no doubt will provide Peking with adequate energy for its own industrial growth—a major factor to consider when assessing China's economic development. It is particularly an advantage to China because it cannot afford to import energy. The petroleum industry will also produce some spin-off effect in terms of the use and development of related industries and technology. And it may prove invaluable in the event that another boycott, like the one following the Korean war, is imposed on China—although this seems an unlikely possibility. Likewise, it would be an important asset in the event of a long period of conventional war. Finally, oil exports are a vital source of foreign exchange, which China badly needs. None of these advantages, however, is significant enough to be regarded as a key to rapid industrialization or modernization in a more general sense. It also must be noted that they have special application to China; other second-ranking powers that are less fortunate in these areas are not necessarily as handicapped as China would be if it did not possess these assets.

In conclusion, China has an edge over the second-ranking powers in all three realms—food, natural resources, and energy—in terms of the amounts of production and in potential production. But this is true in absolute terms only. In per capita terms China ranks below nearly all of the second-ranking powers. China's potential for increasing production of food, resources, and energy is also greater than most other second-level powers—but only slightly, and again not in per capita terms. Thus, in terms of the resource factor of national power, China ranks well above the other second-ranking countries but the absolute nature of this advantage as opposed to a per capita advantage means that it will help China catch up to but not surpass competing powers. Moreover, the application of this asset to international influence, in China's case, is considerably less than the first figures would suggest, due to China's own needs vis-à-vis industrial development. Finally, technology seems to offer solutions to the industrial countries, while rising prices may not have the impact that 1973 seemed to indicate. In short, it appears that China's global role will be affected in a positive way, but only marginally, by its advantages in this area, and that only if the highly industrial second-ranking powers experience serious problems due to resource shortages will China's rank among the hierarchy of powers change. China will probably not be able to close the sizable gap between it and the superpowers in the near future based on its undeveloped resources. In food production, it seems unlikely that it will improve its relative position even over the long run. In fact, a decline may be anticipated. Metal and nonmetal resource production presents the same case. In energy production, China will likely experience some benefits to its international influence because of its endowments. However, these will be limited by the power of OPEC, its own needs, and rapidly increasing exploitation and production in numerous Third World countries.

4

China's Economic Strength

China's economic size clearly ranks it among the major powers. In terms of gross national product (GNP), the usual measure of the size of a nation's economy, China ranks sixth in the world (see Table 4–1). If one considers that GNP is probably not an accurate measure of China's economic strength—measuring it on the low side, since a considerable portion of Chinese production does not enter into office national accounts and therefore is not part of the GNP—and if one also recognizes that GNP figures for industrialized nations are artificially higher, China's rank as a world economic power would be adjusted upward. Furthermore, inasmuch as a comparison is being made between China, which is a developing country and has a tremendous potential for growth, and nations (with the exception of India) that are already mature industrial economies, a more valid, standard comparison might be the growth rate of GNP. If growth figures are examined, China's edge over other top-ranking powers is clear. China's GNP has multiplied several times since

TABLE 4–1

LEADING NATIONS OF THE WORLD BY GROSS NATIONAL PRODUCT, 1976
(billion U.S. dollars)

U.S.A.	$1,890.1
U.S.S.R.	1,047.9
Japan	685.1
W. Germany	514.0
France	381.0
China	372.8
U.K.	246.4
Canada	195.0
Italy	190.6

SOURCE: *Handbook of Economic Statistics* (Washington, D.C.: Central Intelligence Agency, 1978).

1949, when the Communist regime came to power, and has grown much more rapidly than that of such competitors as France, Italy, and the United Kingdom, not to mention the superpowers. Other figures, such as the index of industrial production, steel output, and foreign trade, have shown similar increases (see Table 4–2). None of the other powers with whom China competes for international power status can boast such progress, with the exception of Japan and West Germany, which were devastated by World War II and whose economic growth started at very low figures in 1945.

An estimate of economic strength in terms of the basic ingredients of the national economy—land, labor, and capital—also shows that China outranks the other second-ranking powers by a considerable margin and puts it on a par with the two superpowers. If other factors, such as resources, market size, and scales of production, are considered, the gap is even wider between China and the other second-ranking powers. Added to this, China is self-sufficient economically to a degree similar to the superpowers, while most of the other second-ranking powers, especially those above China on the GNP scale, are not at all self-reliant, as would be demonstrated by economic sanctions, an embargo, or a trade war. A point in fact: the 1973 oil embargo had a direct and serious effect on all the second-ranking powers except Canada, which was influenced indirectly. China was not affected, except in a positive way. Hence, China must be seen as an economic power of quite a different magnitude from the other second-ranking powers with whom it now competes, even from those that are larger in national production terms.

Another factor that should be considered when assessing China's economic strength is that China has a centrally planned economy. Central planning guarantees high investment for future growth and makes possible the building of a heavy industrial base, which, as the Soviet Union has proved, is an excellent model for rapid economic growth. Likewise, China's totalitarian system means that economic strength is directly converted to political or military power. Foreign trade and aid can be directly controlled by the government and used as instruments of foreign policy, and more money can be spent on defense than in competing countries. Consequently, China benefits from a greater amount of influence via equal or comparable economic output capabilities than other nations, with the possible exception of the Soviet Union.

Demonstrating the benefits of planning, China has made tremendous strides in industrial development, building on what was essentially an

TABLE 4–2

China's Major Economic Indicators, 1949–1974

Period and year	GNP	GNP per capita	Industrial production (1957=100)	Steel output (millions of metric tons)	Foreign trade	
					Exports f.o.b.	Imports c.i.f.
	(billion 1973 U.S. dollars)				(billion current U.S. dollars)	
1949–52, Rehabilitation:						
1949	$ 40	$ 74	20	0.16	$0.43	$0.40
1950	49	89	27	0.16	0.62	0.59
1951	56	101	38	0.90	0.78	1.12
1952	67	117	48	1.35	0.88	1.02
1953–57, First Five-Year Plan:						
1953	71	122	61	1.77	1.04	1.26
1954	75	125	70	2.22	1.06	1.29
1955	82	134	73	2.85	1.38	1.66
1956	88	141	88	4.46	1.64	1.48
1957	94	147	100	5.35	1.62	1.44
1958–60, Great Leap Forward:						
1958	113	172	145	11.08	1.94	1.82
1959	107	160	177	13.35	2.23	2.06
1960	106	155	184	18.67	1.96	2.03

1961–65, Readjustment and Recovery:						
1961	82	118	108	8.00	1.53	1.50
1962	93	133	114	8.00	1.52	1.15
1963	103	144	137	9.00	1.57	1.20
1964	117	160	163	10.80	1.75	1.47
1965	134	179	199	12.50	2.04	1.84
1966–69, Cultural Revolution:						
1966	145	190	231	15.00	2.21	2.04
1967	141	180	202	12.00	1.94	1.95
1968	142	178	222	14.00	1.94	1.82
1969	157	192	265	16.00	2.03	1.83
1970–74, Resumption of Regular Planning:						
1970	179	214	313	17.80	2.05	2.24
1971	190	222	341	21.00	2.42	2.30
1972	197	225	371	23.00	3.08	2.84
1973	217	241	416	25.50	4.90	4.98
1974 preliminary	223	243	432	23.80	5.90	6.70

Source: Arthur G. Ashbrook, Jr., "China: Economic Overview, 1975," in *China: A Reassessment of the Economy* (Washington, D.C.: U.S. Government Printing Office, 1975).

agrarian base. The portion of the economy defined as the industrial sector as well as production that enters the national economy have multiplied several times since 1949. The regime has also promoted the development of high-technology industry in a number of areas: nuclear weapons, satellites, petroleum refining, fertilizer production. These and other advanced sectors of the economy stimulate overall growth and serve as a foundation for increasingly rapid economic modernization. Moreover, these industries serve as the basis for specific global influence.

It should also be noted that Chinese leaders not only have been able to engineer industrial development and sustain a high level of overall growth, but have virtually eliminated privation. Most other underdeveloped nations that have experienced rapid economic growth cannot make these claims. Hence, China is an economic model that is emulated by other nations and looked to for advice and guidance. This, together with the fact that there are many Chinese living in other parts of Asia who comprise an entrepreneurial class and maintain ties with Peking, makes China's economic influence beyond its borders considerable, particularly in Asia.

Looking at China's economic power from a more pessimistic or cautious view, most of the arguments above can be discounted considerably as seen in the context of China's economic difficulties and weaknesses. Although China's economic strength is underrated by using the standard of GNP these figures do reflect the external influence or the international importance of a nation's economy. Therefore, without considering other factors, ranking China in terms of GNP is probably a fair reflection of its real economic influence in the global arena. In fact, for reasons that will be discussed below, China's economic power, or its external influence based on economic strength, is less, not more, than its size measured by GNP figures.

As an indication of China's place in the hierarchy of nations based upon GNP, China is outranked by the United States and the Soviet Union in economic power by multiples of more than two-and-one-half and five, and by Japan by nearly double. China is also outranked by two other nations, France and West Germany, while two or three others may be considered close competitors. Thus, the gap between China and the superpowers is greater and its rank among the second-ranking powers lower than the other elements of national power already discussed indicate. On the basis of GNP figures, then, China is a middle-range, second-ranking power and, using this standard rather than other criteria of national strength, there are more second-ranking powers.

When speaking of economic power, like most of the other kinds of power, it is more accurate to speak of blocs or alliances than individual nations. In fact, this is more true of economic strength than of the other categories of national power discussed here. The growing interdependence of nations, based on specialization that increases trade and other economic ties, has increased the importance of regional and other actors in global economic affairs. Because of this, in the event of boycotts or economic warfare, it is unlikely that most nations will stand alone, particularly important powers.[1] Thus, considering that China is not allied with any other nation (again, assuming the Sino-Soviet Alliance is defunct) while most of the other second-ranking powers are, its economic self-sufficiency is not as impressive as it otherwise might be seen to be.[2] Also, when China is compared to various alliance systems, regional systems, and other economic actors, its economic strength clearly diminishes (see Tables 4–3 and 4–4). Under normal conditions, the importance of these nonnational economic actors in terms of global influence is considerable—and their economic strength is increasing faster than China's. During a war, some of them may cease to be meaningful participants in international politics, but probably most of them will continue to play a role, and some of them—such as NATO and the Warsaw Pact—will play a much larger role.

Going beyond economic size in an effort to translate the power of production into international influence, the best measure is foreign trade. Using foreign trade as a benchmark, China's global influence is quite

TABLE 4–3

GROSS NATIONAL PRODUCT OF SELECTED ACTORS

	Million 1974 U.S. dollars	Percent of Planetary Product
NATO	2,721.2	48.9
Western Europe	1,409.8	25.3
NATO in Europe	1,191.2	21.4
European Community	1,129.4	20.3
Warsaw Pact	979.7	17.6
Eastern Europe	270.1	4.9
OPEC	216.2	3.9
China	205.3	3.7

SOURCE: *The Planetary Product in 1974* (Washington, D.C.: U.S. Department of State, November 1975).

TABLE 4-4

GROSS NATIONAL PRODUCT OF MAJOR WORLD ECONOMIC ACTORS COMPARED TO CHINA

	GNP (billion U.S. dollars)	Percent of World GNP
OECD	$3,448.3	62.0%
EEC	1,129.4	20.3
International corporations	350.0	6.3
OPEC	216.0	3.9
China	205.0	3.7

SOURCE: *The Planetary Product in 1974* (Washington, D.C.: U.S. Department of State, November 1975).

small—much less than proportional to its economic size measured in GNP. China does not rank in the top twenty nations, according to the value of its foreign trade, and accounts for less than 1 percent of total world trade (see Table 4-5). In fact, China's foreign commerce clearly categorizes it as a small nation—comparable to Singapore or Taiwan.[3] And it is unclear how fast China's foreign trade will increase in future years. During the 1960s China's foreign trade increased very slowly. From 1970, at the end of the Cultural Revolution, to 1973, the volume increased markedly. After 1974, however, this pattern changed; China's trade increased only slowly, and in 1976 declined by over 9 percent.[4] While the last two years have again witnessed rapid growth, over the last two decades the rate of growth of China's foreign trade has not been as fast as the average growth of international commerce. It is also worthy of note that the commodity terms of trade—in other words, the price of goods China exports compared to prices of the things it imports—have shown an unfavorable trend since 1973 due to the rapid rise in prices of manufactured goods and equipment due to inflation in the industrial countries. China's exports, which consist mainly of agricultural goods, textiles, and crude oil, have not gone up in price so markedly. Hence, China's trade expansion is braked by the fact that the prices of its exports will determine, to a large extent, the quantity of its imports and thus the magnitude of its trade overall.[5] Moreover, a reversal of this trend cannot be anticipated in the near future. Due to the role of technology in pushing up the price of goods China needs to import this may even be a permanent trend.

It is also important to note that China's trade is primarily with the developed Western countries, which means that Peking's influence via

TABLE 4−5

LEADING NATIONS IN WORLD TRADE
(thousand U.S. dollars)

	Value of Exports	Percent of World Trade
U.S.A.	120,101	11.0
W. Germany	118,054	10.9
Japan	81,126	8.2
France	64,997	6.6
U.K.	58,165	5.9
Italy	45,706	4.6
U.S.S.R	45,209	4.5
Netherlands	43,207	4.1
Canada	43,199	4.1
Saudi Arabia	40,894	3.9
Belgium-Luxembourg	37,507	3.6
Iran	24,250	2.5
Sweden	18,766	1.9
Switzerland	17,614	1.8
Australia	13,336	1.3
E. Germany	12,700	1.2
Poland	12,405	1.2
Brazil	12,139	1.2
Nigeria	11,728	1.1
Indonesia	10,853	
Czechoslovakia	10,495	1.0
Spain	10,223	1.0
Denmark	10,223	1.0
Kuwait	10,113	1.0
South Korea	10,047	0.9
South Africa	9,987	0.9
Libya	9,827	0.9
Iraq	9,664	0.9
Venezuela	9,487	0.9
Taiwan	9,349	0.8
Hong Kong	8,526	0.9
Singapore	8,241	0.8
China	7,900	0.7

SOURCE: *Handbook of Economic Statistics* (Washington, D.C.: Central Intelligence Agency, 1978).

commercial ties with other countries in the Communist bloc or the Third World is even less than its overall trade figures would suggest (see Table 4−6). Moreover, China's important trading partners, in terms of volume of trade, are major trading nations; this means that if one side or the other chooses to break the relationship, the impact upon China will be considerably more than upon the other country (see Table 4−7). For example, China's trade with Japan (the only large power that is considered dependent on trade with China or vulnerable to shifts in Peking's trade policies) is more than 26 percent of Peking's total trade; yet, trade with China comprises only 3 percent of Japan's total.[6]

TABLE 4-6

SOURCES OF CHINA'S IMPORTS, 1976
(million U.S. dollars)

Non-Communist countries	$ 4,900
Developed	4,140
Undeveloped	755
Communist countries	1,070
U.S.S.R.	240
Eastern Europe	545
Other*	285
Total	$ 5,975

SOURCE: *Handbook of Economic Statistics* (Washington, D.C.: Central Intelligence Agency, 1977).
*Includes Albania, Cuba, Mongolia, N. Korea, N. Vietnam, and Yugoslavia.

TABLE 4-7

CHINA'S MAJOR TRADING PARTNERS, 1974-1977*

	Percent of Total Trade
Japan	26.8%
Hong Kong	12.1
W. Germany	6.0
U.S.A.	4.2
France	3.5
Canada	3.4
Australia	3.2
Singapore	2.6
U.S.S.R.	2.5
U.K.	2.4

SOURCE: *Asia 1978 Yearbook* (Hong Kong: Far Eastern Economic Review Ltd., 1977).
*Based on total imports and exports.

Foreign economic assistance is another way of translating economic power into international influence. In official aid-giving, China ranks seventh in the world but far below its competitors (see Table 4-8). China's foreign aid amounts to less than 8 percent of France's and just over 2 percent of that given by the United States. Peking's foreign-aid program is exceeded by the fifth largest aid donor, the Soviet Union, by more than five times. Although China has given more aid than its official aid-giving figures reveal, this is more than offset by the fact that Western countries give economic assistance through international organizations and provide important economic benefits to Third World countries through private investments and by giving trade and tariff preferences.[7] In addition,

TABLE 4−8

<small>Official Bilateral Aid Given by Major Nations, 1954−1976</small>
(million U.S. dollars)

U.S.A.	$76,161
France	24,395
W. Germny	13,727
Japan	11,153
U.S.S.R.	11,130
U.K.	9,949
China	2,066

Source: *Handbook of Economic Statistics* (Washington, D.C.: Central Intelligence Agency, 1978).

some of the countries cited that are in the aid-giving business are able to supply food, which is generally regarded as the most influential kind of aid. China makes no donations through international organizations. Selling in the Chinese market is not very meaningful to most countries that are in need of foreign exchange, since China conducts most of its trade via barter agreements and cannot supply many goods that developing countries need. Finally, China cannot give much food aid.

The statistics on foreign investment, another measure of global economic influence, are even more telling. China's investment abroad is almost insignificant—less than one-tenth of 1 percent of the world's total—whereas nearly all the nations that compete with China for national power status are major investors abroad.[8] And, although Peking has eschewed investing in other countries for allegedly ideological reasons, it has extremely meager capabilities to export capital due to shortages at home. Thus, even if China were to change its policy in this regard, it would have very little global impact. The same situation holds true of technology transfers on the basis of sales, joint agreements, or gifts. China's inabilities in the realms of foreign investments and technology sales or transfers also apply to influence in various regional and international organizations that are now important brokers of investment funds and have a significant global influence. China is not a major contributor to any global organization that gives aid or controls trade, technology, or the global money system. Thus, when international monetary matters are discussed, China is usually not invited; elsewhere, it exercises little or no voice.

Another means of measuring China's economic strength as a basis of international influence is to relate it to military strength. Although the military component of national power will be discussed in the next chapter, the reader should note, in this context, that China is not a major supplier of military aid or military technology. Still another measure of economic strength, particularly as it relates to military power, is the level of monetary reserves a country has, defined as gold and other precious metals and convertible currency. Traditionally, this was an important measure of national power, since it enabled a national leader to hire soldiers. Although this is not common today, foreign reserves may nevertheless be cited as an indicator of economic strength since they would be important in the context of global economic instability or protracted international conflict. China's monetary reserves rank it far below at least twenty other nations (see Table 4–9).

Up to this point, the analysis has focused on current economic size and global influence. Since many analysts who take a sanguine view of China's economic power do so on the basis of China's future economic

TABLE 4–9

LEADING NATIONS BY MONETARY RESERVES, 1976*
(billion U.S. dollars)

W. Germany		$38.8
Saudi Arabia		27.0
U.S.A.		18.7
Japan		16.6
Switzerland		13.0
France		9.7
Iran		8.8
Venezuela		8.6
Netherlands		7.4
Italy		6.7
Canada		5.8
Spain		5.3
Belgium		5.2
Nigeria		5.2
Iraq		4.6
Austria		4.4
U.K.		4.2
Australia		3.2
Libya		3.2
U.S.S.R.		2.5
China	(estimate)	2.0+

SOURCE: *Handbook of Economic Statistics*, (Washington, D.C.: Central Intelligence Agency, 1977), except for China.

*The estimate of China's monetary reserves comes from A. H. Usack and R. E. Batsavage, "The International Trade of the People's Republic of China," in *The People's Republic of China: An Economic Assessment*, and *Far Eastern Economic Review*, March 4, 1977, which puts China's gold holdings at $2.46 billion. In view of China's spending abroad over the last two years its monetary reserves have probably decreased recently.

†Includes gold, foreign exchange, and Special Drawing Rights in the International Monetary Fund.

growth, it is necessary to examine in greater detail China's potential. Already mentioned have been the factors of land, labor, and capital as economic assets and reflectors of future growth. As was noted in chapter 2, China is huge in physical size, but its agricultural land area is not proportionally as large. Furthermore, in per capita terms, China is not blessed with large amounts of good land. Thus it was concluded that China cannot become a world exporter of agricultural products and will not be able to depend upon the agricultural sector for sufficient investment funds to guarantee rapid development in other sectors of the economy. The same argument applies to China's natural resources. China is generally well endowed in resources, but not on a per capita basis. Consequently, exports of raw materials have declined due to larger domestic consumption—and another potential means of securing investment capital must be discounted. The other possible asset to be derived from land is location, which favors trade or in some other way accrues economic benefit. Clearly, no special advantage can be cited here.

Looking at China's labor situation, it is immediately evident that China has large supplies of manpower. However, two qualifiers must be juxtaposed with this otherwise favorable situation. First, because of China's intensive agriculture, it needs huge quantities of labor in that sector of the economy. It has been suggested by some writers that for this reason China does not have an excess of labor and even suffers at times from a shortage of manpower.[9] The fact that the Great Leap Forward, instituted in the late 1950s, assumed large amounts of disguised unemployment and underemployment, but failed as an economic development scheme, seems to offer some substantiation for this view. Clearly, as long as China's agriculture is largely labor-intensive—and there is little prospect for a major breakthrough in farm mechanization—this will remain true. Furthermore, China's labor pool is largely unskilled and hence not an unqualified asset to rapid industrial development.[10] Managerial and technical skills are in short supply, especially the latter; and due to the barriers imposed by antiforeignism, the scarcity of translators, and the value placed on self-reliance, it is difficult to utilize foreign sources of training and skill acquisition to alleviate these deficiencies.

In this connection, it should be noted that because of what appears to be an excess of labor—and undoubtedly is, in the sense that there is an oversupply of unskilled workers that seek jobs in the factories—there is little impetus to utilize work-saving methods in industry. Consequently, there is little concern with efficiency. This explains the low productivity

of Chinese industry, which is only one-third that of the Soviet Union and
even less than India's.[11] The lack of concern for labor efficiency, in turn,
acts as an impediment to technological progress in industry. In order to
overcome this difficulty, the Chinese government has employed higher
pay scales for industrial workers and has not allowed free movement into
these jobs. But rural residents are attracted to the cities in search of
higher-paying jobs, and when they are forced back to the countryside
they generate problems that frequently result in economic disruption.
Furthermore, they often return again to the cities to become a cause of
social problems. During the 1960s and early 1970s, factory workers'
salaries were lowered somewhat, in relative terms, to cope with the latter
problem, but this engendered serious labor problems including strikes,
sabotage, and violence.[12] Due to this situation the government allows only
a very low level of labor mobility in China, which exacts costs in both job
satisfaction and innovation.

In the third component of economic growth potential, capital, China
is clearly disadvantaged. China is seriously deficient in capital, even compared to the developing nations.[13] Most less developed countries can
obtain growth capital through foreign investment in the private sector by
Western countries, foreign aid from Western or Communist-bloc nations
(sometimes both, as in the case of India), or from international organizations. The sale of raw products, including agricultural goods, is also an
important source of capital for most underdeveloped countries. In the
1950s, China obtained sizable amounts of capital (not large, however,
relative to China's needs) from the Soviet Union. But as a result of the
Sino-Soviet dispute, this source was cut off in 1960. China has been able
to obtain foreign exchange through Hong Kong, which, in view of the
relationship between Hong Kong and the capitalist countries, may be
seen as a source of Western aid. But China has to earn this money by
supplying goods and services, and the amount is small in relation to
China's needs. The sale of agricultural products and raw materials abroad
provides another source of capital, but this also is small, is declining in
importance, and is now more than offset by the need to import large
quantities of food. By virtue of its tight control over the economy, the
Chinese government can force the accumulation of domestic savings; yet,
because of increasing consumption due to population growth, the base
upon which to extract capital through forced surpluses is small. Foreign
borrowing is a potential source of investment capital, and China's credit is
good; nevertheless, such borrowing presents political problems since it

will no doubt have to be accompanied by greater contacts with foreign countries—which may generate greater expectations and thus greater consumer demands, to the detriment of efforts of the regime to force a greater rate of savings. In fact, this problem has been clearly visible in recent months. Increasing foreign trade is another possibility; and it is now being given a high priority, but it carries with it the same liabilities. Moreover, since China's economic infrastructure is not geared to large amounts of external trade, increasing trade will require a restructuring of the economy as well as considerable investment in building roads and other transportation facilities.

At this point, it is instructive to examine the structure and organization of the Chinese economy in greater depth. It has been argued that China's centrally planned economy gives it an advantage, both in terms of economic growth and in translating economic strength into global influence. That the Chinese economy is rigorously and centrally planned, however, is far from the truth. China is comprised of two, three, or many separate economies, depending upon how one looks at its economic make-up. The most apparent "separate" economy in China is the industrial sector. Industrial areas or zones in China are patently exclusive in terms of location: 50 percent of modern industry is located in three provinces; two-thirds is located in five provinces.[14] Nine industrial cities account for more than 60 percent of China's total industrial production. Industrial areas are also located predominantly on the coast and in the north. As already mentioned in chapter 2, this makes China vulnerable to bombing or to blockade, particularly by the Soviet Union, but conceivably by any naval power. More important in terms of the discussion here, the location of industry signifies that large areas of China are not integrated into the national economy and hence are not affected by national planning. Consequently, China does not possess any real advantage vis-à-vis economic growth based upon scales of production or market size, as would normally accrue to a large country.

One explanation for this situation is China's grossly inadequate transportation system (see Table 4–10). Most goods in China, about three-fourths, are carried by rail. Yet its rail system barely compares with those of the other second-ranking powers that are only a fraction the size of China. West Germany, which is smaller in area than a number of the provinces in China, has more miles of track than exist in all of China. Roads in China, relative to land area, are even more scarce, as are the vehicles to use them. Even compared to India, China has few roads and

TABLE 4–10

World Transportation Facilities of Major Nations

Nation	Vehicular				Rail			
	Roads (km)	Number of Autos	Number of Buses and Trucks	Number of Persons per Vehicle	Tracks (km)	Rolling Stock	Passenger Miles (km)	Cargo Tonnage Miles (km)
U.S.A.	6,002,821	92,082,000	19,928,000	1.8	554,286	1,476,635	17,283	1,134,533
U.S.S.R.	1,358,900	1,650,000	4,600,000	39	135,200	?	265,404	2,633,004
India	1,034,936	606,100	507,500	482	103,768	194,955	3,652	190,695
Japan	1,015,047	7,317,956	8,595,555	6.5	99,995	414,349	113,076	119,856
China	898,000	133,000	480,000	1,239	78,580	330,201	41,040	66,720
Canada	812,159	6,602,200	1,736,000	2.6	72,649	354,910	37,981	73,544
France	784,739	12,800,000	2,904,000	3.2	60,000	?	?	301,000
W. Germany	415,000	14,376,500	2,523,400	3.6	50,912	424,706	35,712	21,972
U.K.	358,781	12,455,000	1,755,000	3.9	48,931	198,205	288,854	62,472

| | Air | | | Merchant Marine | | | | | Inland Waterway | | |
Nation	Number of Airports	Passenger Miles (km)	Cargo Tonnage Miles (km)	Nation	Vessels Over 1,000 Gross Tons	of Which Tankers Number	Total Dead Weight Tonnage (000)	Cargo (000 metric tons)	Nation	Canal Mileage (km)	Cargo Tonnage Miles (km)
U.S.A.	4,260	218,544,000	7,179,936	Japan	2,153	388	44,900	477,812	China	200,000	74,000
U.K.	140	18,668,500	541,131	U.S.S.R.	2,059	419	14,957	158,600	U.S.S.R.	144,500	165
Canada	136	17,245,000	522,259	U.K.	1,713	451	40,673	252,545	U.S.A.	41,006	448,000
India	62	3,616,000	125,976	U.S.A.	1,372	291	19,634	511,042	India	14,000	?
Japan	53	16,155,000	397,000	W. Germany	958	69	12,545	138,237	France	8,623	14,183
France	47	14,064,000	558,392	France	450	134	10,000	192,885	W. Germany	5,981	47,800
U.S.S.R.	38	78,500,000	2,070,000	India	249	13	3,918	50,009	Canada	3,050	?
W. Germany	18	8,604,000	573,792	China	237	27	1,659	?	U.K.	1,457	131
China	?	?	?	Canada	60	16	273	253,127	Japan	?	108,800

SOURCE: *Encyclopedia Britannica*, 1975.

motor vehicles. The United States, which is smaller than China, has seven times the length of roads and more than two hundred times as many vehicles to use them.[15] The same is true of sea and air transport. Only in the use of canals is China ahead of most other countries, and this does not make up for its lack of capabilities elsewhere.

Because of the lack of roads and vehicles, more than one-third of the villages in China are, for purposes of economic integration, inaccessible. The counties, and even in many cases provinces, constitute isolated, self-reliant economies.[16] Inadequate transportation facilities thus limit the advantages to be gained from the division of labor and specialization, while hampering technology dispersion and use. This, in turn, results in a serious duplication of effort in developing new techniques or products, and limits gains from comparative cost advantages and broader resource utilization.[17]

Another problem that belies the claim that the Chinese economy is centrally controlled is its uneven development. In China, there are large gaps in the economy resulting from the overdevelopment of one sector of the economy while others lag. Due to the size of these gaps, the stimulants to overall growth provided by advanced, progressive industries or developed sectors of the economy, such as China's nuclear program, are minimal. Similarly, there is little spin-off effect, and technological development in one industry does not generally foster advances in other industries, as happens in Western countries.[18] This is true even in the areas in which resources and funds are committed in large quantities because of needed inputs from other advanced sectors of the economy. For example, China has made impressive strides in missile propulsion, but its missiles are not the high-quality weapons they should be, due to guidance problems stemming from insufficient computer capabilities. Such problems characterize China's advanced industries and are also typical of the economy as a whole.

To rectify this situation, China needs better transportation and communications systems, a much more effective system of economic controls, and simply a more effective government to promote and coordinate economic development. Considerable evidence suggests that China's slow (by the standards of stable developing nations) and uneven economic growth is largely the product of poor planning and the inability of China's leaders to design rational growth policies and carry them out.[19] At present, Peking's major efforts to encourage growth fall primarily into the category of exhortation and verbal encouragement. This does not confirm that China has a totalitarian, controlled economic system or, if it does, that it is an asset to economic development.

At this point, it is useful to examine in greater depth the magnitude and nature of China's industrial development. This process is enlightening in terms of validating the negative impact of the problems cited above and also in projecting China's international economic influence in the future. Inasmuch as industrial strength is more relevant to global influence than economic growth per se, it is also a better indicator of China's economic power in the global arena.

The first three years after the Communist takeover constituted a period of rebuilding, marking the end of a long period of economic dislocation and stagnation. In these years, as well as those that followed, China accrued important benefits from the Soviet Union in the form of credits, technology, and preferential trade. During the period from the end of 1949 to 1953, essentially a period of rehabilitation, industrial production increased at an annual rate of 34 percent; after 1953, industry expanded at a yearly rate of 16 percent.[20] However, by 1957, the effects of over-investment in the industrial sector to the detriment of the agricultural sector appeared. As a consequence of trying to link the two sectors of the economy, together with mismanagement and poor planning during the Great Leap Forward, industrial growth dropped drastically. Due to the dearth of statistics, it is uncertain how serious the decline was, but from 1960 to 1962 it was marked. And recovery was slow. The 1964–1965 period saw some growth, but the Great Proletarian Cultural Revolution (1966–1969) reversed the forward progress once again. Looking, then, at the period from 1958, when the first five-year plan ended, until 1972, which represents a peak year in recovery after the Cultural Revolution, China's industrial growth rate averaged around 6 percent—the same as India's during that period and considerably less than that of most other developing countries. China's industrial growth during that period also lagged behind that of other second-level powers such as France, Japan, and West Germany.[21] During the early 1970s, there was another spurt in industrial growth based upon increases in foreign trade, foreign borrowing, and the importation of complete sets of machines, factories, and technology. But by 1976 the growth in industrial production began to level off.

A pessimistic or optimistic view of China's industrial production record from 1949, like its economic growth overall, thus depends upon what period is considered. If the entire period is used, growth figures are quite impressive. However, the decline is quite marked (growth, in recent years, is about one-fourth of early increases). Hence, if one uses the entire period and considers only increases in production, the decline of industrial growth is so marked that projected future growth rates would be predictably very small. If one measures from the end of the period of economic rehabilitation, the declines in industrial productivity increases are much less and would not be considered serious; but the growth rate maintained is not very impressive when compared to that of other developing nations. Nor is it large considering the size of the gap between China and the two superpowers. Therefore, when using industrial growth as a measure of China's economic strength, one must categorize China as a nation that, like Japan and Germany, suffered serious destruction during the war. Rapid growth during the rehabilitation phase was not then so much the product of sagacious planning and the utilization of important economic assets; rather, it reflected the ending of a period of economic dislocation. In China's case, however, industrial growth was not maintained during the late 1950s and the 1960s, due to the necessity to improve agriculture and because of various structural problems already mentioned.

In order to relate the problem of China's industrial development to future economic growth, and especially to China's world power status, several sectors of the economy need to be analyzed in greater depth. One of China's major industries, the steel industry, illustrates China's economic problems as they relate to future industrial growth and therefore can be taken as a case study.[22] It should also be recalled that the potential of China's steel industry has been the basis for some very optimistic predictions regarding China's future national power status, and that in the 1950s the regime, following Stalin's model of development, devoted a high level of investment to the steel industry and has since given it a preferred status in development plans.

China is blessed with large deposits of iron ore and coal, the two basic ingredients in steel production. However, most coal deposits, as already noted, are low in quality. The same is true of most of China's iron ore deposits; thus, benefaction processes are required. Due to the low level of technological development and the investment costs involved, China's coal and iron ore have largely gone unused. Other difficulties have also hampered the growth of China's steel industry: Mao's efforts to decentralize the industry in the late 1950s, the pull-out of Soviet technicians and the cut-off of aid in 1960, and the assault on skilled workers and managers for their "capitalist road" tendencies during the Cultural Revolution.

Due to the above-cited problems, steel production in China in the early 1970s barely equalled that of the early 1950s. Meanwhile, demands increased, forcing China to import more than a million tons yearly from Japan. At present, China is the fifth nation in the world in steel production, but with an output less than one-fourth that of Japan (see Table 4–11). Moreover, that ranking is maintained by importing coke, scrap iron, and machinery for steel production from Western countries.

In order to make further prognostications concerning China's future economic development and to relate its economic strength, both present and future, to world power status, it is necessary to look at some more general statistical data and try to determine its significance. It is also useful to look at China's economic problems and prospects in the context of the competition. In this way, a meaningful hierarchy of economic powers can be constructed.

China's overall economic growth, like its industrial development, is quite impressive if 1949, the date the Communist government was established, or even 1953, the beginning of the first five-year plan, is used as a starting point. On the other hand, the decline in the growth rate suggests zero or negative growth in coming years (see Table 4–12). If 1955 is used, economic growth is not as rapid nor is there a significant slowdown in growth. Using 1955 or 1956 as a starting point probably provides a more accurate picture of China's economic growth as it will look in coming years: growth will continue but rates of expansion will be

TABLE 4–11

LEADING NATIONS IN CRUDE STEEL PRODUCTION, 1977
(million metric tons)

U.S.S.R.	147.0
U.S.A.	113.2
Japan	102.4
W. Germany	39.0
China	25.0
Italy	23.3
France	22.1
U.K.	20.4
Poland	17.8
Czechoslovakia	15.1
Canada	13.7

SOURCE: *Handbook of Economic Statistics* (Washington, D.C.: Central Intelligence Agency, 1978).

TABLE 4−12

China's Long-Term Economic Indicators
(percent)

Item	1953−74	1958−74
GNP	5.6%	5.2%
Agricultural production	2.4	2.0
Industrial production	10.5	9.0
GNP per capita	3.4	3.0

SOURCE: Arthur G. Ashbrook, Jr., "China: Economic Overview, 1975," in *China: A Reassessment of the Economy* (Washington, D.C.: U.S. Government Printing Office, 1975).

TABLE 4−13

China's Gross National Product Growth Rate Compared to the World Average
(percent)

	1955−60	1960−65	1965−70	1970−74
China	3.8%	3.9%	5.2%	4.7%
World	4.5	5.0	5.4	4.7

SOURCE: *The Planetary Product in 1974* (Washington, D.C.: U.S. Department of State, November, 1975).

moderate and will compare to the world's average as they have in the recent past (see Table 4−13).

When comparing China's economic development to that of the powers with which China will compete for global influence, one again gets mixed results. China has made gains on the United States and the Soviet Union if growth figures are used, no matter what the base year. In absolute economic size, however, the gap between them and China has grown. In comparison to the other second-ranking powers, China increased its relative rank after 1949 but later fell back. During the 1950s China moved up in rank among the world's economic powers and in 1957 was in fifth place in terms of GNP. However, in the 1960s China fell to seventh place. In the mid-1970s Peking moved back up to sixth place.[23]

Recent economic growth figures indicate similar conclusions. In 1975, agriculture in China grew by 2 percent, or slightly faster than population growth. In 1976 it experienced no gain. Industry grew by 10 percent in 1975, but failed to grow at all in 1976. Thus, GNP growth rates for 1975 and 1976 are 6.8 percent and 0.2 percent, respectively.[24] The average for the two years was 3.5 percent, or slightly below the world's average. Economic growth in 1977 was higher, about 8 percent in terms of GNP, thus bringing China's growth for the period 1975–1978 to above the world's average.[25] But based on past trends and the fact that China is now basing growth upon the importation of plants, machinery, and fertilizer and is going into debt to do so, these recent, rather impressive growth figures probably cannot be sustained.

In conclusion, China's economic development has been fraught with various problems, and the rate of its future economic growth is uncertain. Development in China depends upon reducing population growth; yet China's world-power status, and certainly its large standing military force, depend upon a large population. Growth would be facilitated by giving greater emphasis to the industrial sector, but the demand for more food due to a high birth rate precludes diverting investment from agriculture. An alternative would be to import grain on a large scale and permanent basis from the West. However, this would make China very dependent upon several countries that have grain for export. Peking would probably be well advised to increase its trade with the Western industrial countries (which it is now doing) so as to increase labor specialization and facilitate technology importation and utilization; but this will mean sacrificing self-reliance, or autarchy, while it will constrain China's trade, and thus its influence, with the underdeveloped nations of the Third World. In short, China's economic growth seems to depend upon policies that will reduce its global economic influence.

In terms of global economic influence China is a low ranking second-level power. When its economic strength and influence are compared to various military and regional economic actors, China's size is even less impressive than when comparisons are made with the superpowers and other second-ranking nations. Prognostications of the future suggest little improvement. China's economic strength may grow vis-à-vis the superpowers, but Third World countries and regional actors will increase their economic size and influence as fast or faster than China.

5

China's Military Power

China's military strength has been one of the most common grounds upon which it has been judged a major power and perhaps even a superpower. And this estimate is not totally unfounded. China compares with the two superpowers in some facets of military strength, and in some ways exceeds them. In a host of ways, China is militarily superior to the other second-ranking powers. Two of the most frequently cited are the size of China's army and its nuclear capabilities. China is also an historical military power, and its leaders seem to have the willpower to play such a role once again. Perhaps most important, China has demonstrated its military prowess against both the United States and the Soviet Union—the only second-ranking power to do so.

By other criteria of measuring military power, China is not a military giant. It does not possess a broad range of military capabilities and has little capacity to use its military, save by strategic bombing or nuclear missile attack, more than 200 or so miles beyond its borders. Its air force and navy lack many important capabilities, and its military machine generally suffers from lack of sophisticated weapons and weapons systems. Finally, China has no allies of importance.

Following is a more in-depth analysis of China's military strengths and weaknesses. The reader should keep in mind that an attempt is being made, as in previous chapters, to measure China's capacity to play the role of a major international actor. Thus, global military influence is given greater emphasis than regional or defensive capabilities.

In terms of military manpower, China ranks as the world's largest standing military force (see Table 5–1). If reserves are counted, China's lead increases. If militia, security forces, and other military and submilitary organizations are added, China outranks other competitors several-

TABLE 5-1

MILITARY PERSONNEL IN SELECTED NATIONS

China	4,325,000
U.S.S.R.	3,638,000
U.S.A.	2,068,800
India	1,096,000
France	502,800
W. Germany	489,900
U.K.	313,253
Japan	240,000
Canada	80,000

SOURCE: *The Military Balance, 1978–79* (London: International Institute for Strategic Studies, 1978).

TABLE 5-2

COMBAT AIRCRAFT IN THE AIR FORCES OF SELECTED NATIONS

China	5,200
U.S.S.R.	4,600
U.S.A.	3,400
India	670
France	557
U.K.	550
W. Germany	509
Japan	364
Canada	210

SOURCE: *The Military Balance, 1978–79* (London: International Institute for Strategic Studies, 1978).

fold.[1] In fact, its military manpower, broadly defined, exceeds the total populations of either superpower and any of the second-ranking powers except India. China is similarly a top-ranking military power judging by the size of its air force and its navy, using the number of aircraft and ships as a standard. China has the largest air force in the world in terms of number of planes (see Table 5–2). Its navy is also the largest in terms of the number of ships and is frequently ranked third by other standards (see Table 5–3). Using the criterion of military expenditures or defense budgets, China ranks third among the world powers (see Table 5–4).

In strategic weapons, China may be judged to rank easily above the other second-ranking powers. In fact, Peking is often regarded as the only serious contender with the superpowers for nuclear status.[2] The United Kingdom is a nuclear power, but its delivery systems and its strategy are tied to the U.S. defense establishment in such ways as to make the British less than an independent force. Moreover, its nuclear arms-

TABLE 5–3

MILITARY SHIPS OWNED BY SELECTED NATIONS

China	1,504
U.S.S.R.	445
U.S.A.	251
U.K.	164
W. Germany	158
Japan	138
France	125
India	72
Canada	41

SOURCE: *The Military Balance, 1978–79* (London: International Institute for Strategic Studies, 1978).

TABLE 5–4

LEADING NATIONS BY DEFENSE EXPENDITURES
(billion 1978 U.S. dollars)

U.S.S.R.	130.0
U.S.A.	115.2
China	35.0
France	17.5
W. Germany	17.2
U.K.	13.0
Iran	9.9
Saudi Arabia	9.6
Japan	8.6

SOURCE: *The Military Balance, 1978–79* (London: International Institute for Strategic Studies, 1978).

building is diminishing, and no attempt is being made to keep pace with developments made by the United States or the Soviet Union. France is more an independent nuclear power, but it also has abandoned any effort to compete with the superpowers and is declining in strategic weapons' force level vis-à-vis the United States and the Soviet Union. India is a nuclear power, but has only tested a device, not a bomb, and has foresworn building nuclear weapons. Furthermore, New Delhi has not tested a missile designed to deliver a nuclear warhead.

In contrast, China has tested various kinds of nuclear weapons, increasing in terms of size and sophistication since 1964, when it first became a nuclear power. It has built both atomic and hydrogen bombs and has tested various warheads from both planes and missiles. China now has probably 300 nuclear weapons stockpiled, ranging in size from 20 kilotons to 3 megatons.[3] It possesses 60 medium-range bombers and 400 short-range bombers, in addition to more than 50 medium-range missiles and 30 intermediate-range missiles. Finally, Peking is building intercontinental ballistic missiles and submarine-launched missiles, both capable of carrying nuclear warheads, and probably will have these operational soon.

Strengthening the argument made regarding China's military capabilities, it must be noted that China is an historical military power—the only significant historical power in East Asia. By virtue of its current military strength and the expectations of its neighbors, Peking holds sway over most of Asia—the world's largest and most populated continent. The capacity of the Chinese army to literally saturate a number of border countries makes them, in many respects, vassal states or at least buffer zones. Japan and India are the only other regional powers, and neither can counter China's military strength at any level.

China's experience in various conflicts and wars since 1949 can be offered as further proof that China is the dominant military power in the region, while it is also evidence that China's military is experienced and combat-tested. In Korea, Southeast Asia, and in confrontations with Taiwan, India, and the Soviet Union, the Chinese defense establishment proved itself while it gained valuable fighting experience. Chinese military commanders have likewise demonstrated their ability to fight various kinds of conflicts, ranging from guerrilla war far from China's borders to conventional war, and even to engage in limited conflict with a superpower. Equally important, Chinese leaders have shown their mettle and have won for their country the reputation of a major world power from both friends and enemies.

The most convincing evidence that China is a major military power is the fact that first the United States and now the Soviet Union have tried to contain China militarily, but with little success. Moreover, China has been the cause of weakening both U.S. and Soviet military influence abroad—through the Vietnam War and the Sino-Soviet dispute. Finally, both have built weapons systems aimed at the Chinese military threat and continue to design and build with China in mind. Certainly, no other nation can make such a claim.

On the other hand, China's strengths must be qualified when its military capabilities are put into the context of contemporary global political realities, including the existence of alliance systems and the growth of military power in the Third World. In addition, it must be noted that China's military strength is hampered by various kinds of weaknesses and problems which only deeper probing and analysis reveal.

Although China is a leading military power by virtue of having a huge standing military force and vast quantities of personnel in reserve forces and other military and submilitary organizations, its military manpower is not so large considering the long land and sea borders it has to defend. Given its insecure frontiers, China's army is probably not larger in terms of its needs than that of other second-ranking powers.[4] The main reason a number of these powers do not maintain larger armies is the fact that secure borders and the absence of proximate hostile powers make it unnecessary. In addition, China has no allies, while most of the other second-ranking military powers are allied with each other, and all of them with one of the superpowers. Finally, when comparing China's military manpower force levels with the two major military alliance systems, its advantage, even in manpower, disappears (see Table 5–5).

The figures on China's military manpower are also deceptive in several other ways. First, the Chinese army is employed for building roads and other public works. It does not devote itself full-time to military activities. Second, the reserve and militia are large because some military training is given to almost all adult citizens in China who are not too old or are not handicapped. However, many of them do not train with weapons, or they use wooden guns. Many practice only a few hours a year. Also, as we will see later in this chapter, the Chinese military is not well equipped, and many of its weapons are small or obsolete. Larger stores of manpower are needed to compensate for this fact. Third, China maintains a large military force to use in case of internal disorder, which also serves as a base of political power, a socializing organ, and a means of controlling unemployment.[5]

The size of China's military budget makes China the world's third-ranking military power, but it is much smaller than the allocations of the superpowers for defense. Using this criterion, China is not a superpower,

TABLE 5–5

MILITARY PERSONNEL IN MAJOR MILITARY ALLIANCE SYSTEMS COMPARED TO CHINA

NATO	4,825,800
Warsaw Pact	4,732,000
China	4,325,000

SOURCE: *The Military Balance,* 1978–79 (London: International Institute for Strategic Studies, 1978).

but rather a high ranking second-level power. This is even more clearly the case when low estimates of China's defense expenditures are used.[6] Low estimates put China's defense spending at about the level of West Germany, France, the United Kingdom and Iran.[7] Then when comparisons are made between China's defense expenditures and those of the two major alliance systems, China's budget looks quite small. Using high estimates, China spends around 20 percent of either NATO's or the Warsaw Pact's budget (see Table 5–6).

It is unlikely that this situation will change in the near future. Due to the need for investment in economic growth, China cannot afford larger defense bills. In order to avoid the high costs of building defense industries, China may seek to buy more weapons and weapons systems abroad. In fact, Peking has made some important purchases from the United States and the United Kingdom in recent years, including jet engines, computers, and radar systems.[8] However, it has been estimated that China will need to import $100 billion in weapons in the next five years to develop a credible deterrent force against the United States or the Soviet Union, and this would mean increasing China's national debt to 50 percent of its GNP—clearly unrealistic in view of the pressure on the Chinese leadership to invest more in economic development and the production of consumer goods.[9] Reliable sources of sophisticated or high-technology weapons constitute another problem. Certainly, Washington will not sell China the weapons it needs to attain a credible offensive force against the United States. And it is unlikely that Washington will allow those of its allies whose arms sales it can control to do so either. It is even more unlikely that the Kremlin will sell such weapons to China, since they would be targeted against the Soviet Union. There are no other sources of the highly advanced weapons.

TABLE 5–6

DEFENSE EXPENDITURES OF MAJOR MILITARY ALLIANCE SYSTEMS COMPARED TO CHINA
(billion U.S. dollars)

NATO	184.1
Warsaw Pact	139.0
China	35.0

SOURCE: *The Military Balance, 1978–79* (London: International Institute for Strategic Studies, 1978).

An examination of the kind and quality of weapons possessed by China's air, naval, and land forces also reveals very serious weaknesses in China's military strength and equally serious limitations in terms of translating military power into global influence. China's air force has a large number of aircraft, but most are not combat aircraft. Also many are obsolete Soviet-built MiG 17s and MiG 19s that are badly in need of repair.[10] China possesses between 50 and 200 MiG 21s and a somewhat larger number of home-built F-9s. However, Peking has experienced production problems with the F-9, and it is reported that production of this plane has slackened in recent years.[11] In any case, all of China's fighter interceptors are lacking, or show weaknesses, in three important areas: all-weather capability, air-to-air missiles, and missile-avoidance equipment. China's fighter bombers have an operating radius of only 300 to 500 miles, limiting their use to the region. Its bomber fleet is patently obsolescent: 100 TU-16s that have a top speed of less than 600 miles per hour (about the same as ordinary commercial jet aircraft now in use). They do not carry defensive weapons of any sophistication, or jamming or other equipment to avoid ground-to-air or air-to-air missiles. Peking apparently realized that this plane was out of date in 1974 and suspended production, but it has not begun production of a replacement long-range bomber.[12] China has no intercontinental bomber and is not currently working on one. Other weaknesses of the Chinese air force include lack of communications equipment, almost no close air support weapons, limited airlift capabilities, and no air-refueling capabilities, overseas bases, or aircraft carriers.

Considering the above-cited deficiencies, the Chinese air force clearly has little utility beyond a few hundred miles of China's borders. Because of the emphasis on missiles and the high cost of building better aircraft, along with the lack of needed military technology, it is unlikely that this situation will change soon. A number of other nations have better fighting capabilities in the air, including several European countries, two or three Middle East nations, and probably India and Japan.

A similar situation applies to China's navy. It is large in quantitative terms because it has a large number of patrol boats and because even small craft of the junk-size belong to the naval forces.[13] However, China has few ships that can operate long distances from Chinese waters. In terms of major surface combat vessels, China does not compare favorably to the other second-ranking powers (see Table 5–7). It has fewer destroyers than Japan, France or Italy. Unlike India and Australia, it has

TABLE 5–7

U.S.S.R.	214
U.S.A.	176
U.K.	76
France	52
Japan	47
India	32
Spain	27
Canada	23
Italy	21
China	18
Netherlands	18
Taiwan	18
W. Germany	17
Brazil	16
Turkey	14
Australia	13
Greece	13
Argentina	12
Chile	11
Venezuela	11

Source: *The Military Balance, 1978–79* (London: International Institute for Strategic Studies, 1978).

no aircraft carriers.[14] Its amphibious forces are similarly weak. Its strength is in submarines, but these are chiefly older vintage craft that can be detected easily; and the number does not equal one-half of those in service by the United States or the Soviet Union. Furthermore, offsetting its strength in undersea warfare, the Chinese navy is seriously handicapped by deficiencies in antisubmarine warfare equipment, especially sensing and tracking devices. The Chinese navy's nuclear capabilities are similarly a telling weakness: China has one nuclear submarine; the United States has 70 and the Soviet Union has 40.[15] And its single nuclear submarine cannot fire nuclear-tipped missiles or fire while submerged. In fact, the Chinese navy has no nuclear-weapons capability at all. United States and Soviet submarines fire mirved (multiple independently targeted) missiles from under water. France also has this capability.

China's navy is useful for coastal defense but not much more than this. It has no overseas bases and few, if any, refueling points which could be guaranteed in wartime; hence, it has virtually no sustained operational capabilities in distant waters. And like the air force, naval armaments-building in China is slow, signifying little likelihood that the status quo will change. Peking certainly cannot fill the naval vacuum in South and Southeast Asia, particularly in the Indian Ocean.

The Chinese army is comprised of 160 divisions, almost all of them ground forces.[16] Only seven are armored. Chinese tanks are almost all older and slower Soviet-built models. Many are of World War II vintage. Chinese armored capabilities, judging from the number of divisions and the quality of equipment, are less than those of Egypt, India, Israel, the United Kingdom, and West Germany. Antitank weapons are also few in number and are considered out of date by standards used by other middle-ranking powers. The Chinese army is similarly deficient in logistical, transport, and communications capabilities. Since neither the air force nor the navy can provide these, Chinese military leaders face serious handicaps in moving troops quickly over long distances. Consequently, most army divisions are assigned permanently to one area of China and cannot be relocated. In short, the Chinese army is limited to effective operation not more than 100 miles beyond its borders.

A number of other problems can be cited relative to the effectiveness of the Chinese army as a fighting force. There is a great deal of provincialism in the Chinese army, which means that it may be difficult to use many units for anything except home guard even in the event of a border war. As recently as 1971, there was a major threat of rebellion and even secession on the part of regional military commanders.[17] Morale is also a question. The army leadership was seriously demoralized after the Korean War by high casualties and the effectiveness of napalm and air power against its mass-invasion tactics. Subsequently, army leaders made demands for bigger and better weapons and more professionalism. But China could not afford these things, and friction between military and civilian leaders resulted. This occurred again after the Cultural Revolution, at which time officers close to former Defense Minister Lin Piao were purged. Tensions between the Army and the Party have been evident since that time. In short, conflict seems to be inherent in civilian-military relations in China, while there is resistance by regional military commanders to the authority of national military leaders. This clearly presents an obstacle to unity and, in some cases, may preclude effective action against an external enemy.[18]

In addition to its conventional forces, China has developed strategic weapons—namely, nuclear weapons and missile delivery systems—and these have been commonly flaunted as the basis for China's great power status. However, despite fairly rapid progress, China is still far behind the two superpowers in both areas. The exact number of warheads possessed by each is uncertain, but a rough estimate would put those of the

United States and the Soviet Union at around 10,000 compared to about 300 in the hands of the Chinese.[19] A count of missile delivery vehicles possessed by each again puts China far behind the superpowers and even behind France and possibly the United Kingdom (see Table 5−8). In weapons-related nuclear technology, China trails far behind the super-powers and probably lags behind France and the United Kingdom by a fairly sizable margin—an observation made by military experts in the West and confirmed by the number of nuclear tests conducted by each (see Table 5−9). In nonweapons nuclear technology, based upon the development of nuclear power plants, China is behind several more nations, including Belgium, Israel, Japan, Norway, Sweden, and West Germany.[20]

The utility and effectiveness of China's strategic weapons may also be doubted. China's nuclear weapons have virtually no utility at all against

TABLE 5−8

MAJOR POWERS BY NUMBERS AND KINDS OF STRATEGIC WEAPONS

	Intercontinental Ballistic Missiles	Medium and Intermediate Range Ballistic Missiles	Submarine Launched Ballistic Missiles	Bombers (long-range, modern)
U.S.S.R.	1,477	620	909	135
U.S.A.	1,054	−	656	441
France	−	18	96	−
U.K.	−	−	64	−
China	−	60–80	−	−

SOURCE: *The Military Balance, 1978−79* (London: International Institute for Strategic Studies, 1978).

TABLE 5−9

NUCLEAR TESTS CONDUCTED BY MAJOR POWERS*

U.S.A.	614
U.S.S.R.	354
France	64
U.K.	27
China	21
India	1

SOURCE: *World Armaments and Disarmament SIPRI Yearbook* (Stockholm: Stockholm International Peace Research Institute, 1977).

*as of January 1, 1977.

targets in the United States, since Peking needs an intercontinental ballistic missile or a long-range bomber with air refueling capabilities to
reach the mainland United States and does not possess either.[21] Even
when it builds these, U.S. defense systems probably will be able to nullify
China's threat for some years. The European powers and Canada are
also out of range of Chinese delivery systems. Most of the Soviet Union is
within range of Chinese medium-range and intermediate-range missiles
and bombers; however, it is questionable whether or not China could
inflict much damage on the Soviet Union.[22] Moscow has perfected satellite reconnaissance so that it can locate Chinese missile sites, and it has
over-the-horizon radar to pick up firings immediately. With rapid com-
puterized trajectory plotting and a larger number of defensive missiles
than China has offensive missiles, the Soviets may be able to stop most or
all of them in flight. Soviet fighter planes will certainly be able to stop
Chinese bombers before they reach their targets. The Soviets' intelli-
gence-gathering capabilities and advanced work on lasers and other high-
technology defense weapons may ensure that Peking does not attain
unacceptable destruction capabilities vis-à-vis the Soviet Union in the
foreseeable future.

Another weakness is China's air defense system, which consists mainly
of early warning and control radar linked to interceptor aircraft and
several hundred ground-to-air missiles. China's radar system is regarded
by experts as inadequate to deal with low-flying bombers or aircraft using
penetration aids. The entire system lacks computerization, and total reaction time is no doubt too slow to cope with incoming missiles. In any
case, China's defensive missiles are not sophisticated or large enough in
number to reduce significantly a missile attack by either superpower.
China probably also would have difficulty reacting to missiles or super-
sonic aircraft launched from an aircraft carrier or submarine by a second-
ranking power.[23]

China's strategic weapons might be used to threaten Japan or India or
any of the smaller countries of Asia. However, Japan has a defense agreement with the United States that guarantees it nuclear protection. India
has the same with the Soviet Union. In the case of most border nations,
the problem of fallout blowing back on China limits the use of nuclear
weapons considerably and, consequently, the credibility of such a threat.
China has little or no tactical nuclear capabilities to compensate for this.
In addition, the two superpowers have jointly signed a pact with provi-
sions in it affording protection by U.S. and Soviet nuclear weapons to

nonnuclear states that are threatened by any nuclear power. Perhaps even more important, the use of nuclear weapons by China would result in tremendous political costs in terms of national prestige. Hence, the threat of nuclear weapons on China's part is not a major facet of the military balance anywhere in the world, not even in Asia.

China's nuclear power status clearly has not given Peking the international prestige which Chinese leaders no doubt expected when they embarked upon efforts to develop nuclear weapons and delivery systems. In fact, China's nuclear status may be seen as counterproductive, since it has caused a number of Asian nations to ally with the United States or the Soviet Union, or at least welcome their presence in Asia and seek their nuclear protection. It has also evoked regional military cooperation in Southeast Asia, which may be a crucial factor in the region's military situation in years to come. For these reasons, plus the fact that China cannot possibly catch up to the superpowers in strategic military power, the rapid progress China made in nuclear weapons-building during the 1960s and early 1970s is not very relevant to its global influence. Also, it is slowing down. Considering the lower priority Peking is now giving to nuclear weapons, together with its criticism of the arms race and its statements that China will never be a superpower, one might speculate that it is opting out of the nuclear arms contest.

China's global military influence is limited for still other reasons. During the 1960s Peking was able to cause considerable trouble for the United States, as well as for the Soviet Union, by supporting "people's wars" or wars of national liberation in Third World countries. These efforts, however, brought little benefit to China. When conflicts in underdeveloped areas expanded to become limited or conventional wars, China showed little ability to win influence due to its military's inability to operate in areas distant from China or in conventional war settings. In the Middle East, Bangladesh, and Angola, China lost rather than gained influence. Elsewhere, its gains have been temporary or have brought few rewards, or both. Hence, China's global strategy changed during the early 1970s, giving little emphasis to encouraging and supporting revolutionary movements.[24] At the present time at least, Peking has abandoned its former global military strategy—one which many observers saw as the basis for a major Chinese global role.

Another reason for China's meager military influence abroad is its inability to provide military aid to other countries. The Chinese military assistance program is overshadowed by those of the superpowers and is exceeded by several European countries (see Table 5–10). Compared to NATO and the Warsaw Pact, China's military aid is minuscule—less than 1 percent of the two combined (see Table 5–11). Furthermore, in most areas where China has supplied arms, it has brought a reaction from either Washington or Moscow, often to the disadvantage of the recipient. As a consequence, most Third World countries are reluctant to ask for Chinese military aid.[25]

This brings us to question China's historical role as a military power and thus to its natural position of military dominance in Asia. Historically, China was occupied or controlled by other countries, especially those to the north, much of the time. In modern times, China suffered defeats at the hands of the European powers and Japan, the Soviet Union incorporated land claimed by the Chinese, and other smaller powers made territorial demands upon China. The main reason that China is considered by many to be a regional power is that Japan's military strength

TABLE 5–10

MAJOR ARMS-EXPORTING NATIONS*
(million U.S. dollars)

	1955–77		1977
U.S.A.	50,265	U.S.A.	6,785
U.S.S.R.	21,040	U.S.S.R.	3,265
U.K.	4,950	France	890
France	4,675	U.K.	700
W. Germany	2,525	W. Germany	550
Italy	1,380	Italy	265
China	695	Belgium	120
Belgium	525	China	65
Switzerland	280	Spain	40
Netherlands	265	Switzerland	25

SOURCE: *Handbook of Economic Statistics* (Washington, D.C.: Central Intelligence Agency, 1978).
*Figures include military sales, down-payments, and military aid.

TABLE 5–11

ARMS EXPORTS BY MILITARY BLOCS, COMPARED TO CHINA, 1955–1977
(million U.S. dollars)

NATO	65,820
Warsaw Pact	23,780
China	695

SOURCE: *Handbook of Economic Statistics* (Washington, D.C.: Central Intelligence Agency, 1978).

was reduced to almost nothing after World War II and most of the nations on China's periphery at the close of World War II were militarily weak. However, in recent years, both Japan and India have been increasing their military spending at a pace exceeding China's. During the period 1972–1976, Japan doubled its defense budget to become the world's seventh strongest military power.[26] Since the mid–1960s India has increased its spending on defense more than China. Finally, almost all of the countries on China's periphery are now supporting large military forces and have allied directly or indirectly with either the United States or the Soviet Union. Thus, the notion of a power vacuum in Asia, especially Southeast Asia, that China can exploit is no longer real.

China's mettle as a military power is also subject to discounting. This point is discussed at greater length in the next chapter; however, it should be noted here that although China has been involved in a number of wars in the last nearly three decades they can hardly be considered wars of aggression on China's part.[27] In Korea, China may have been forced into the war by the Soviet Union. It certainly did not commit troops until U.N. forces neared Chinese territory. In 1962, China committed what appeared to be aggression against India, but disputed territory was involved and Peking sought only limited objectives. During the Vietnam war, China never provided troops for combat use. In its confrontation with Vietnam in 1979 China pursued only limited objectives and took action only after Vietnam invaded China's protégé, Kampuchea. Conflicts with Taiwan have been very limited in scope, and Taipei continues to hold island fortresses a few hundred yards off China's shore. Chinese leaders have spoken recklessly about nuclear weapons, but their cautious actions belie their true attitudes.[28]

The combat experience of the Chinese military is likewise not as much a valuable asset as an initial perception might suggest. In no major conflict in which China has engaged since 1949 has either the Chinese air force or navy been involved more than superficially. Thus, neither can be regarded as truly combat-experienced. The army has gained considerably more experience, but much of this does not apply very well to most present-day situations. The combat-training gained in Korea is too out-dated to be of much value. Border conflicts with India and the Soviet Union did not provide much experience in mobile warfare, the use of coordinated air-land efforts, or sophisticated planning; and only a small portion of the Chinese army was involved in each of these. The conflict with Vietnam in 1979, during which regular Chinese forces fought Vietnamese militia and local force, seems to prove the inadequacy of the Chinese army's experience: In the initial phase of the conflict the casualty ratio was almost even, although the Chinese army was pitted against Vietnamese reserves and militia units.

Related to this point is the commonly held view that China was responsible for a deterioration of the military strength of both the United States and the Soviet Union—due to the Vietnam war and the Sino-Soviet conflict. Indeed, the United States reduced its military manpower level after Vietnam as well as its defense budget. Its alliances with a number of nations were weakened, and a number of temporary allies and neutrals became skeptical of American military strength. On the other hand, America's Vietnam problem was largely the product of its own mistakes. And, clearly, Soviet aid to Hanoi was more important than Chinese aid; it exceeded China's by a large margin and was crucial to the final victory. Another point is also important in this connection: the relative decline of America's military role started long before the Vietnam war; Vietnam simply signified a turning point in the ending of Washington's international policeman role. And although America's military presence abroad has diminished, the global strategic balance has not changed.

It is also true that the Soviet Union has withdrawn a large number of troops and weapons from Europe and that its military presence there is not as formidable as it once was. Its control over its Eastern European satellites has weakened. But this was also part of an already existing trend and there has been no serious escalation in the form of independence movements, save in Czechoslovakia where the Kremlin demonstrated its resolve and crushed the effort to attain greater independence. Despite Moscow's retreat from Europe, the balance of power there still favors the Soviet bloc in terms of manpower, armor, and other conventional weapons. Meanwhile, the Kremlin has increased its defense spending in strategic weapons and naval power. In both areas Moscow has made considerable progress, making it a significantly stronger power in most respects than it was a decade ago. The Soviet Union is certainly more a global power than it was prior to the Sino-Soviet dispute and doubtless a bigger threat to Chinese interests. Clearly, Moscow poses a larger obstacle to Peking's influence in Asia and the Third World than it did five, ten or fifteen years ago.

China's role in altering the world military-power balance, then, must be regarded as exaggerated. It is also something that was largely fortuitous. Had the Vietnam war occurred elsewhere, the credit redounding to

China would have been minimal. In any case, it is quite certain that these events will not repeat themselves and that their effect is a matter of the past and present, not the future. Thus, the reputation China gained should be regarded as accidental, and no doubt it will soon diminish. This seems to be the case already in Southeast Asia.

In summary, China must be regarded as a major military power in that it has formidable conventional warfare capabilities, especially if an attack were made on its own territory by a second- or third-ranking power. It also has a considerable capacity to support wars of national liberation or guerrilla wars. Finally, it is a nuclear power. However, all of these assets must be qualified. China's conventional capabilities are limited to proximate areas due to the Chinese military's limited logistical capabilities. Likewise, the Chinese military would not be an effective fighting force in a conventional war with either superpower, assuming that either escalated the conflict quickly. Peking's capabilities to start, augment, or support wars of national liberation are considerable, but are now trammelled by the fact that nations that consider asking for China's help must expect the United States or the Soviet Union to aid their adversaries. Furthermore, Peking, in attempting to become a recognized legitimate world power, has abandoned, to a large extent, the use of the strategy of wars of national liberation. Finally, China's nuclear status is offset by the fact that either superpower could literally obliterate China in a nuclear exchange, but China could not do the same in return. Then China's global influence based on its nuclear status is reduced in significance by the realization that nuclear weapons cannot be used without serious political repercussions and the fact that since nuclear status is now so easy to attain it is no longer regarded as the mark of a major military power.[29]

These qualified strengths must also be juxtaposed with the weaknesses in China's military capabilities already mentioned, and its larger military needs than those of other nations. In addition, in the global arena China is not just competing with other nation-state actors; it is also competing against alliance systems. And although there is some evidence that the world's alliance systems may change, this must be regarded as a long-range forecast; even if this happens, it is unlikely that it will have much effect on China's global military role. Finally, there will remain the contradiction between China's aspiration to superpower status, or even the status of a special second-ranking power, and an alliance with either superpower. Hence, China is probably destined in the foreseeable future to play a similar role to the one it is playing now.

6

The Chinese Political System, Diplomacy, and Will

Many political analysts cite the well-organized and efficient political system in China, Peking's astute diplomacy, and the will of Chinese leaders as important assets when assessing China's power status and its role in international politics. Indeed, China does seem to possess strengths in all of these realms, particularly when comparisons are made with the past. Furthermore, a brief examination of several thousand years of Chinese history reveals that China was weak when it lacked unity or was ruled ineffectively. Similarly, its diplomacy contributed to its strengths and weaknesses or mirrored them very accurately. The same is true of the abilities and ambitions of China's rulers. In short, in the past when China was well managed politically and its leaders had the will to rule an empire, China dominated its known world. This, so it seems, may be true again.

In 1949 Mao and his followers established a political system in China that was vastly different from anything China had known in the past: a Communist-totalitarian regime. The new system provided China's leaders with a means of unifying the country and establishing national purposes. Its ideology was a futuristic and highly goal-oriented one, and it amplified Chinese nationalism which Mao had already inspired. A single political party—the Communist party—monopolized political power and made decisions that allowed for neither dissent nor opposition. The party controlled police power as well as the press and the educational system. Representing total and centralized control it promised to transform China immediately from a weak nation to a powerful one.

The success of China's new polity was also mirrored by the growth of the party from a relatively small, elite group to an organization that by

1969 was the largest organized political party in the world. The victory over the Nationalists in 1949, and subsequent campaigns to change the system of land tenure and eradicate landlordism, also proved that the party could fully mobilize the population and had mass support. Social and political change that followed further demonstrated this fact; so did national economic planning. The capabilities of the regime to maintain control over a huge population were likewise shown in its ability to run the media and the educational system and vastly increase the size and effectiveness of both. Even some age-old facets of Chinese society were changed: the Chinese language was simplified, the literacy rate increased, and almost everyone was given a basic education and provided with news-type reading materials during and after their educational years.

Meanwhile, the top hierarchy of the Chinese leadership demonstrated a consensus on purposes and policies that no other leadership in China has possessed in recent years, if ever. In fact, Chinese leaders appeared to be more in agreement on basic goals than governments of other major countries. Provincialism, which was a serious problem in the past, seemed to be overcome, allowing Peking to establish more control over a larger number of people than any other regime on earth.

As a result of political stability at home, in addition to its potent ideology, which espoused a clear and ambitious world view, China ended a long period of isolationism. China joined the Communist bloc and formed a military alliance with the Soviet Union. In this way, Peking compensated for its past seclusion and dearth of experience in world politics, as well as its lack of allies and modern weapons of warfare. So doing, it gained the ability to confront U.S. and U.N. forces on the battlefield in Korea. Subsequently, Peking engaged successfully in a diplomatic battle with the West by overcoming the U.S.-inspired economic boycott against China and by winning diplomatic recognition abroad despite Washington's efforts to contain and isolate China. Later, China began to win over neutral nations in Asia and Africa, and not just in the realm of trade and ambassadorial ties. Peking also won a position of leadership of various revolutionary movements throughout the world. Meanwhile, it undermined the international reputation and role of the United States by winning a psychological victory over the United States in Vietnam while contending with the Soviet Union for leadership of the Communist bloc. Capping these trends, in 1971 China won admission to the United Nations—in spite of American opposition. In fact, it won by a sizable majority, with the support of nations in every part of the world. In so doing

Peking now has a permanent seat on the Security Council, which represents the five most powerful nations in the world, and with it a veto over all important United Nations decisions.

Moreover, Peking is a leader in the U.N. General Assembly, where China, in promoting the cause of the Third World, has rallied a majority of the nations of the world behind its leadership on a host of important issues. It may be said that China is the de facto leader of the Third World and other poor and underdeveloped nations. Inasmuch as the United Kingdom and France are members of the U.S. bloc, while the Soviet Union is considered a rich nation by many Third World nations, China clearly represents a third force that competes with both superpowers. And this bloc of poor countries, in terms of population, land, and natural resources, is much larger than the other two. Thus, China has established itself as a proponent of a new style of international politics that is no longer dominated by the superpowers. Here Peking seems to be riding the wave of the future.

While accomplishing all of this, Chinese leaders have clearly manifested the will to be a world power. They have shown the courage to engage the superpowers in war—the United States in Korea and Vietnam, and the Soviet Union on their common border. They initiated a war against India, which China won easily, and on a number of occasions have intimidated Japan. They have built atomic weapons and delivery systems despite an international ban on testing and efforts by the nuclear powers to stop nonnuclear countries from building such weapons. In addition to providing leadership and aid to national liberation movements, China has an active foreign aid program that has included more than 60 nations on five different continents. All of this adds up to the conclusion that China is a nation that can and desires to be a major power.

In contrast to this optimistic but popular view of the immense contribution made by China's polity to its national power capabilities, there is an equally strong counterargument that its political system does not contribute to global influence, and that negative aspects of its foreign policy and global ambitions offset the positive aspects. The effective rule of China by the Chinese Communist party can be questioned for a number of reasons. First, although the party grew quite rapidly up to 1964, during the late 1960s the membership declined, and during that time the authority of the party clearly diminished.[1] Hence, the argument that the party has steadily increased its control and that political power in China has become more and more centralized is, at minimum, questionable.

Even before the Cultural Revolution, when Mao nearly decimated the Chinese Communist party, the party did not monopolize political power; it shared it with the government and the military. In short, there were, and still are, three bases of political power in China, maybe more.[2]

Second, and perhaps more important than the disparate bases of political power, is the problem of bureaucracy in all political institutions in China, especially the party. Throughout the 1950s and 1960s, Mao criticized the party as an elite, ossified organization, which, rather than providing for a smooth line of political communication, served as an obstacle.[3] It was partly for this reason that he promoted the Great Proletarian Cultural Revolution, during which he organized Red Guards and other youth groups and radicals to tear up the party in the name of removing those "power holders taking the capitalist road." To Mao, destroying the party was the only solution to the problem of bureaucratism.

After the Cultural Revolution, China was run at the top by Mao's personal followers; elsewhere, it was administered primarily by "revolutionary committees"—comprised of the military, former party personnel, and mass-organization (Cultural Revolutionary) people. In essence, China had a new political system.[4] After the Cultural Revolution, there was no effort to centralize political control after the fashion of the 1950s. In fact, China was reorganized politically into six "Great Administrative Regions"—an administrative system employed prior to 1954.[5] At present China's political system is still undergoing change, hence, it is uncertain whether it is suitable to present conditions or is still undergoing a trial period.

It is also questionable whether or not the party has the support of the masses in China. First of all, it is worthy of note that the composition of the Chinese Communist party is not representative. For example, while the party claims to speak for the entire nation and especially the workers and peasants, the number of members of peasant origin is low. Women, also, are not represented well. The military is overrepresented in the party, but its influence is subject to a high degree of fluctuation; so is that of the educated elite. Regional favoritism is also obvious.[6] There is similarly reason to question party solidarity and, therefore, the unity of the ruling hierarchy in China. Careful analysis reveals that there has been serious factionalism in the party since the Communists came to power in 1949, resulting in the periodic purging of top leaders: from Kao Kang in the early 1950s to Peng Teh-huai in the mid-1950s, Liu Shao-ch'i in the late 1960s, Lin Piao in the early 1970s and the "Gang of Four" in the late

1970s. Teng Hsiao-p'ing and Hua Kuo-feng now appear to represent opposing factions. In fact, a history of party in-fighting suggests that factionalism is endemic in the Chinese Communist party and there seems to be no immediate remedy.[7] In short, China's political leadership does not reflect that the nation is unified or that the regime has popular support.

Related to factionalism in the party, and in part its cause, is the argument over the so-called "two lines"—political purity versus competence, or revolutionary fervor versus pragmatism. This dichotomy pervades Chinese politics and represents basic or fundamentally different attitudes toward communism as well as the means of attaining it.[8] It also involves disparate views concerning the best formula to engineer economic growth, and it relates to relations with the Soviet Union—which itself constitute a deep-seated controversy within the Chinese leadership. It seems similar to and as much endemic to China as the tensions between rich and poor in capitalistic societies. Certainly, it creates the same or more serious centrifugal tendencies and apparently has no easy solution.

Provincialism also has been, and continues to be, a problem in China despite the party's highly centralized organization. During every political crisis or period of instability in recent years, regional leaders have taken prerogatives that formerly belonged to the party center or to the national government. Even during periods of stability, local authorities frequently have acted on their own and defied central party or government directives. As a corollary, many leaders at the center maintain their positions in the party by serving as spokesmen or advocates of provincial leaders.[9] During the Cultural Revolution, local and regional military leaders assumed more than half of the positions in the central government, and most of the administrative duties in the countries and special districts. They gave their loyalty to regional commanders of one of the four or five armies that have dominated Chinese Communist military affairs from the 1930s.[10] It appears, then, that there is a fundamental contradiction in the Chinese polity between authoritarianism and a strong central government on the one hand and the tradition of provincialism and local self-government on the other.[11] Mao tried to bridge this gap through a populist leadership and through his personal charisma; however, the fact that by his own admission he frequently did not have the support of the masses tends to cast doubt upon the effectiveness of his style of rule.

The fact that since the Cultural Revolution there have been frequent changes in basic ideological tenets suggests that ideology is in a state of flux.[12] Perhaps communism in China needs to undergo further evolution and change. Alternatively, the importance of ideology in China may have been exaggerated as a means to legitimate political control and rationalize the political system. Clearly, China is still in search of an adequate political form to fit its needs.[13] Some scholars even question whether or not there exists a political system (or ideology) that can effectively rule a country as large and diverse as China while it remains essentially economically underdeveloped.[14] Hence, perhaps more important than questioning whether or not the Communist-totalitarian model fits China, one may ask if China has implemented such a model.

Statistical data are offered below to answer the question of whether or not China is a totalitarian regime and at the same time make possible some comparisons with political control and stability in competing nations. One of the marks of a totalitarian regime and, for that matter, a measure of the development of any polity, is effective political communications.[15] Totalitarian regimes typically control the mass media and increase its size and pervasiveness. However, the media in China is not as pervasive as in most other countries. Of the nations we have considered as competitors of China for world-power status, only India ranks lower in terms of the per capita circulation of newspapers (see Table 6–1). Looking at the world as a whole, China ranks in the lower one-third in newspaper readership.[16] A major reason, of course, is the low level of literacy in China, which remains low by world standards in spite of the massive efforts of the regime to teach everyone to read and write. One way of overcoming this obstacle is by using the spoken word. However, of the major contending powers, China is also low (in fact, ranks last) in terms of radios per capita (see Table 6–2). And in television receivers on a per capita basis, China is

TABLE 6–1

NEWSPAPER COVERAGE IN SELECTED NATIONS
(circulation per 1,000 population)

Japan	511
U.K.	463
W. Germany	399
U.S.S.R.	336
U.S.A.	302
France	238
Canada	215
China	19
India	14

SOURCE: *Encyclopedia Britannica,* 1975.

TABLE 6-2

RADIO COVERAGE IN SELECTED NATIONS
(persons per receiver)

U.S.A.	0.7
Canada	1.3
U.S.S.R.	2.6
W. Germany	3.1
U.K.	3.1
France	3.2
Japan	3.9
India	45.0
China	91.0

SOURCE: *Encyclopedia Britannica*, 1975.

ahead of only India, while ranking in the lower 5 percent on a world basis[17] (see Table 6-3). Hence it is highly doubtful that the government has truly established an effective means of communication in China.

A totalitarian regime also requires a centralized and pervasive police system that imposes thought control on the populace, in the same manner that any polity depends upon effective law enforcement. It is doubtful to what extent China has a pervasive police system that operates by directives from the central government. Mao did not try to establish a terror police organization such as existed in the Soviet Union under Stalin, probably in large part because of his inability to do so. Whether or not the means exist in China to carry out thought control in the Soviet sense is uncertain. In fact, the very existence of an effective central police authority is subject to some speculation. The national police organization is not pervasive in Chinese society, as is shown by the fact that it

TABLE 6-3

TELEVISION COVERAGE IN SELECTED NATIONS
(persons per receiver)

U.S.A.	2.2
Canada	2.8
U.K.	3.3
W. Germany	3.5
Japan	4.3
France	4.5
U.S.S.R.	7.0
China	2,532.0
India	25,574.0

SOURCE: *Encyclopedia Britannica*, 1975.

has not been used by leaders to purge opposition factions.[18] Moreover, during the Cultural Revolution, the army had to take over many police functions from the Ministry of Public Security. This produced a high level of decentralization of police power.[19] Some recentralization has been accomplished since the Cultural Revolution, but the degree is uncertain. At present, it does not appear that China has a highly effective national police or security system, especially considering China's large population and the fact that around 4 percent of the population is officially defined as "class enemies." Furthermore, it is clearly not as large as it needs to be considering that millions of youths are dissatisfied with the regime and are banished to the countryside only to return to the cities later without authorization.

Therefore, it would appear that several important means of political control, and thus the means to centralize political authority, are absent or weak in China, and the system must rely on exhortation rather than compulsion. Total control of the population is far from an established fact and probably will not be realized in the near future. What is more, China is still, in many ways, an underdeveloped state politically. In fact, political development in China may be behind most of the rest of the world. Some empirical data on political stability, which will afford some comparisons between China and other nations competing for global status, are useful. These data may be questioned in terms of their relevance or even whether or not political stability is a sine qua non for global influence. Nevertheless, they do reflect what is generally termed the effectiveness of government.

Figures that encompass the early part of the Cultural Revolution, but not the violent stage, show that China outranks all competitive powers in the number of organized internal armed conflicts as well as in general domestic violence (see Table 6–4 and 6–5). In the frequency of armed conflict, here defined as groups using weapons and violence against another group or against the government, China ranked fifth in the world behind only Algeria, Indonesia, Malaysia, and South Vietnam. In the second category, which comprises general violence and resulting deaths, China ranked eighth in the world, following only Algeria, Angola, Hungary, Indonesia, North Vietnam, Rwanda, and South Vietnam.[20] It may be argued that the Chinese political system intentionally perpetrates such kinds of violence or that it is typical of underdeveloped countries. However, comparing the number of riots in China with the number in other Communist countries, most of which are not catego-

TABLE 6–4

ARMED CONFLICTS IN MAJOR POWERS, 1949–1967

China	1,906
India	1,672
U.S.A.	902
France	535
Italy	214
Canada	113
W. Germany	89
U.K.	45
U.S.S.R.	43
Japan	35

SOURCE: Charles L. Taylor and Michael C. Hudson, *World Handbook of Political and Social Indicators* (New Haven: Yale University Press, 1972).

TABLE 6–5

DEATHS FROM DOMESTIC VIOLENCE IN MAJOR POWERS, 1949–1967

China	21,000
India	5,016
U.S.S.R.	399
U.S.A.	318
France	111
Italy	96
Japan	28
W. Germany	9
U.K.	9
Canada	8

SOURCE: Charles L. Taylor and Michael C. Hudson, *World Handbook of Political and Social Indicators* (New Haven: Yale University Press, 1972).

rized as highly developed and all of which have similar political systems, China still shows a high degree of instability and lack of government control (see Table 6–6). In fact, using this criterion, China must be considered the most unstable of any of the Communist bloc governments. Although these statistics are biased in that China experienced a period of widespread internal turmoil during the Cultural Revolution from 1965 to 1970, similar movements have produced violence since then—such as the "criticize Confucius–Lin Piao campaign" and the movement purging the "Gang of Four"—suggesting that considerable cause for unrest still exists in China.

In conclusion, inasmuch as China is a closed system, or at least tries to be, its leaders can avoid allowing the outside world to know about its

TABLE 6-6

RIOTS IN COUNTRIES WITH COMMUNIST GOVERNMENTS, 1949-1967

China	190
Poland	68
E. Germany	67
U.S.S.R.	44
Czechoslovakia	43
Romania	25

SOURCE: Charles L. Taylor and Michael C. Hudson, *World Handbook of Political and Social Indicators* (New Haven: Yale University Press, 1972).

internal problems, which, therefore, appear to be less severe than they actually are. This is an advantage in that it alleviates domestic dissatisfaction with the regime by shutting out external causes of dissent and protest. On the other hand, when China opens up, which it appears to be doing now, and the Chinese masses gain access to the outside world, they will doubtless make greater demands upon the government for both political freedom and material comforts. And, since the world is rapidly growing smaller and interaction among nations and peoples is increasing, others may conclude that the Chinese political system is incongruous and must change—and when that occurs the Chinese government will be exposed to tremendous outside pressure.

While, in some respects, it represents marked changes from the past, China's diplomacy, using objective standards, cannot be considered either successful or intense; nor can it be deemed compatible with the requirements of the modern world. Since 1949, China has been isolated much of the time by its own volition. It has also alienated many nations in the international community by its diplomatic conduct and its nuclear testing, while its exclusiveness, ideology, and political system have engendered opposition, or at least apprehension, in many other foreign nations. Furthermore, the fact that the primary goals of Chinese foreign policy have changed a number of times and Peking has continuously been at odds with at least one of the superpowers, suggests that its diplomacy is a trial-and-error one and that China is still trying to formulate a suitable external policy.

Peking's diplomacy seems intense in large part because of its practice of sending large missions abroad and because the Communist Chinese— due to their dress, ideology, unique behavior, and the fact that they have not been seen abroad much in the past—draw attention to themselves.

Also, after 1949 the West, and later the Soviet Union, tried to keep China out of the international arena, which made Chinese diplomatic efforts even more noticeable, particularly when successful. However, the record of Chinese diplomacy, when compared with that of competing superpowers and second-ranking powers, reflects that Peking has not been and is not now diplomatically more active than other second-ranking powers. Furthermore, whether or not external relations will afford the rewards which Chinese leaders expect and need in order to sustain a more active foreign policy than they are used to, is uncertain. There are many among the Chinese leadership who oppose greater foreign involvement. Then, it must be questioned whether or not Peking's new and more legitimate international role will give it much global eminence. Peking has sacrificed considerable influence among Third World revolutionary countries by seeking better relations with the United States. Meanwhile, its relations with the Soviet Union remain bad and, as a result, the Kremlin takes every opportunity to undermine China's diplomacy.

Again, some comparative statistics are revealing. Using the number of treaties signed with other nations as a measure of diplomatic activity, China ranks sixth in the world behind the two superpowers, the United Kingdom, France, and West Germany. However, many of these agreements are treaties of friendship and are thus more facade than proof of a broad and comprehensive diplomacy. China ranks much lower in diplomatic and military agreements (see Tables 6–7 and 6–8). This reflects clearly that China has few friends or allies and must usually act alone in the global political arena. It also mirrors a continued isolation, which can

TABLE 6–7

DIPLOMATIC TREATIES SIGNED BY SELECTED NATIONS, 1976

U.S.S.R.	354
U.S.A.	324
France	277
U.K.	243
W. Germany	233
Italy	177
Japan	115
China	104
Canada	72
India	40

SOURCE: Peter H. Rohn, *Treaty Profiles* (Santa Barbara, Calif.: Clio Books, 1976).

TABLE 6–8

MILITARY TREATIES SIGNED BY SELECTED NATIONS, 1976

U.S.A.	563
U.K.	137
France	86
W. Germany	74
Italy	70
Canada	65
Japan	43
U.S.S.R.	42
India	18
China	7

SOURCE: Peter H. Rohn, *Treaty Profiles*, (Santa Barbara, Calif.: Clio Books, 1976).

be explained only by inexperience, lack of will, or other nations' distrust and dislike of China.

Since 1949 China's foreign policy has gone through various ups and downs, but even during times of extroversion or diplomatic offensives, China must be regarded as the most isolated of any first- or second-ranking powers. The years 1964–1965, for example, may be regarded as a period of intense diplomacy. Yet China was least represented abroad of any major power (see Table 6–9). In fact, it tied with Venezuela in the position of 41st among 132 nations polled.[21] During the Cultural Revolution, China was, with no doubt, the most isolated of any second-ranking or even third-ranking power in the world, with only one ambassador at his post and most of its embassies abroad either shut down or doing business on a priority or emergency basis only. In Peking, most

TABLE 6–9

DIPLOMATIC MISSIONS SENT ABROAD BY SELECTED NATIONS, 1964–1965

U.S.A.	100
France	98
U.K.	96
W. Germany	88
Italy	87
Japan	71
U.S.S.R.	65
India	64
Canada	55
China	38

SOURCE: Chadwick F. Alger and Steven J. Brams, "Patterns of Representation in National Capitals and Intergovernmental Organizations," *World Politics*, 1967.

foreign embassies and consulates reduced their staffs, and foreign diplomatic personnel maintained little contact with Chinese officials. In the wake of the Cultural Revolution, China gave a new emphasis to foreign affairs and sought to be a more legitimate world actor. But its success has been limited by its bad relations with the Soviet Union and Soviet bloc countries as well as with countries that have been traditionally hostile to China or are anti-Communist.

One serious obstacle to its greater success in the global arena that deserves special attention is the quality of China's diplomatic personnel. In China, ideological standards are rigidly applied to the admission of students into schools that train diplomats and in deciding promotions within the foreign ministry. Thus, there is less concern with merit than with ideological purity. Moreover, this concern over ideological background has engendered struggles and purges in the foreign policy-making apparatus, particularly during the Cultural Revolution when nearly half of the top personnel in the foreign ministry were purged.[22] Another problem is that students who are training to be diplomats or government officials do not have good exposure to international news. They obtain access gradually, and this slows down their training process. Similarly, training in Marxism-Leninism and the thought of Mao takes much time, and, furthermore, causes Chinese diplomats to interpret international events in an ideological rather than an objective context. A third problem is that language training, until recently, was given little emphasis; now, foreign languages are taught, but usually mechanically and without any realization of the need to study foreign cultures as a part of language training.[23] The most important international language, English, has been and remains seriously neglected in terms of both teaching and use. Undoubtedly, it is for these reasons that few Chinese are able to win influential positions in the United Nations or other international organizations (see Table 6–10).

China has been admitted to the United Nations and has been given great-power status as a member of the Security Council. But so far China has not been active in U.N.-related affairs, as is reflected in its membership in U.N.-related organizations and the number of treaties it has signed with the United Nations and other international bodies (see Tables 6–11 and 6–12). Since winning representation in the United Nations in 1971, Peking has been generally cautious and reserved. According to its own admission, this is a product of its inexperience and lack of understanding of U.N. procedures.[24] Another reason is the Sino-

TABLE 6–10

IMPORTANT PERSONS IN THE UNITED NATIONS AND
RELATED AGENCIES BY SELECTED NATIONS

U.S.A.	555
U.K.	351
France	259
India	151
W. Germany	123
Canada	103
U.S.S.R.	90
Japan	65
China	31

SOURCE: *Who's Who in the United Nations and Related Agencies* (New York: United Nations, 1975).

TABLE 6–11

TREATIES WITH UNITED NATIONS BY SELECTED NATIONS, 1976

U.S.A.	127
U.K.	39
Italy	20
India	16
Japan	15
France	13
U.S.S.R.	7
W. Germany	5
China	1

SOURCE: Peter H. Rohn, *Treaty Profiles* (Santa Barbara, Calif.: Clio Books, 1976).

TABLE 6–12

TREATIES WITH INTERNATIONAL ORGANIZATIONS OTHER THAN
UNITED NATIONS BY SELECTED NATIONS, 1976

U.S.A.	557
U.K.	355
Italy	156
France	148
Japan	123
W. Germany	120
Canada	94
India	87
U.S.S.R.	56
China	3

SOURCE: Peter H. Rohn, *Treaty Profiles* (Santa Barbara, Calif.: Clio Books, 1976).

Soviet dispute. Open and often embarrassing disagreements with Soviet leaders in the United Nations have manifestly reduced China's appeal to Third World countries, and in the minds of many U.N. representatives have branded Peking as radical and inflexible. Although Peking is sometimes a leader of causes of Third World countries, it shows little promise of winning permanent leadership of this disparate group of nations for a variety of reasons, among them the Third World's need for trade assistance and technology and its symbiotic relationship with the rich countries, the appeal of nonalignment, and the role of competing leaders in regional affairs. In fact, the record of its U.N. diplomacy suggests that China may be led by, rather than leading, Third World countries.[25]

Further assessing China's diplomacy, it must be repeated that China has virtually no allies. It has had alliances with Vietnam and Albania, but they, in addition to the Sino-Soviet alliance, are now practically speaking defunct. China had an alliance with Kampuchea and depending upon one's interpretation may have one with North Korea. But none of these are of value to China. China is at odds with both superpowers, and has regarded (and to some extent still regards) the other two Asian powers, Japan and India, as enemies. Finally, Chinese diplomatic practices and Peking's interpretation of international law are seen by most other nations as unorthodox; to date no nation has accepted China's style of participation in international politics, and few nations sympathize with Chinese practices.

In short, China is in a situation in which it must make many changes and adjustments in order to increase its diplomatic influence. However, these changes will be difficult. Peking no doubt will be able to improve its diplomatic position somewhat in coming years; but it will face many competitors. It is unlikely that it will make significant progress vis-à-vis most of the other second-ranking powers. Clearly, it is not to be expected that China will make much headway in winning a position of leadership of the poor nations, inasmuch as most of its own trade is with the rich nations, and most of the poor countries remain reliant upon the developed nations or the United Nations for aid.

Measuring the willpower of Chinese leaders or the Chinese people is very difficult, but it is quite clear that an accurate reading cannot be based upon its leaders' statements or policy proclamations. Moreover, China's threat to the international system has been patently exaggerated by the United States and other Western nations, thus presenting an inflated view of the will of Chinese leaders and their nation. What follows may not give a very accurate picture of China's willpower as a nation, or even afford a good comparison with other nations; but it will help formulate a view unencumbered by nationalistic statements, irredentism, or proclamations about war or threats of military action—all features of official Chinese rhetoric. Moreover, the standards used here are objective and have been applied by other scholars to measure a nation's willpower.

One standard that is commonly thought to reflect the will of the leaders of a nation as well as its populace is the amount of the national budget it spends on its military. Using this standard, China ranks high; in fact, China rates near the superpowers and above all competing second-ranking powers (see Table 6–13). This, however, must be seen against the fact that China's gross national product is lower, and therefore it must spend more proportionally. Also, as has been noted already, since China has no allies and because of the many nonmilitary functions that the military performs in China it naturally spends more on defense. Finally, it is relevant that the percentage of GNP devoted to the military in China has declined considerably—from 15.8 percent in 1968 to around 11 percent in 1975 to 6.4 percent in 1978.[26] During this period, most competing nations increased their defense spending in relative terms.

Some alternative measures of willpower that use military preparation as their bases are the percentage of the population in military service and the amount of military aid. By percentage of population in the military, China ranks in sixth place among major powers but far below the top five (see Table 6–14). In arms exports, China ranks far below the superpowers and well below four other second-ranking powers (see Table 6—

TABLE 6–13

PERCENTAGE OF GROSS NATIONAL PRODUCT DEVOTED TO
MILITARY SPENDING IN MAJOR NATIONS

U.S.S.R.	12.7%
U.S.A.	7.4
China	6.4
U.K.	5.4
France	4.4
W. Germany	3.7
Canada	2.5
Japan	0.9

SOURCE: *World Military Expenditures and Arms Transfers* (Washington, D.C.: U.S. Arms Control and Disarmament Agency, 1978).

TABLE 6-14

SIZE OF ARMED FORCES IN RELATION TO POPULATION
SIZE IN MAJOR NATIONS
(military personnel per 1,000 population)

U.S.S.R.	14.06
France	9.54
U.S.A.	8.97
W. Germany	7.98
U.K.	6.15
China	3.48
Canada	3.39
Japan	2.13
India	1.56

SOURCE: *World Military Expenditures and Arms Transfers* (Washington, D.C.: U.S. Arms Control and Disarmament Agency, 1978).

15). Using these two standards, China would have to be classified as a low-ranking, second-lead power.

Another quantifiable measure of a nation's willpower is its foreign aid. Chinese leaders have demonstrated a great amount of determination to play a role in world affairs by giving foreign aid. In fact, China stands out as the only underdeveloped country that is in the foreign aid business.[27] On the other hand, the amount of aid China has given does not compare favorably with either superpower or with France, Japan, the United Kingdom, or West Germany, as was noted in chapter 4. This is even more true of foreign aid as a factor of GNP. Using this standard China is low compared to other second-ranking powers (see Table 6-16) and even compared to a number of small Western powers and the OPEC nations. Since China is the only poor country in the group, this may be

TABLE 6-15

ARMS EXPORTS BY MAJOR NATIONS, 1970-1976
(billion U.S. dollars)

U.S.A.	$25.5
U.S.S.R.	12.2
France	2.4
U.K.	2.1
W. Germany	1.6
Italy	0.7
China	0.4

SOURCE: *World Military Expenditures and Arms Transfers* (Washington, D.C.: U.S. Arms Control and Disarmament Agency, 1978).

TABLE 6-16

PERCENTAGE OF GROSS NATIONAL PRODUCT GIVEN IN
FOREIGN AID BY MAJOR NATIONS, 1976

France	0.711%
Canada	0.580
U.S.S.R.	0.536
W. Germany	0.394
U.K.	0.320
U.S.A.	0.315
Japan	0.216
China	0.037

SOURCE: *Handbook of Economic Statistics* (Washington, D.C.: Central Intelligence Agency, 1977).

an unfair comparison. Nevertheless, it is a factor that measures a nation's will.

Finally, the number of diplomats sent abroad can be taken as a measure of China's ambitions. Because China is still not accorded diplomatic recognition by a number of nations and is not as active in the United Nations as it probably will be in coming years, this measure may underrate China. However, inasmuch as Peking finds it difficult to send diplomats to many places due to specific restrictions not applied to other countries or to Communist nations only, China is handicapped. Also, it should be kept in mind that during the Cultural Revolution, most of China's diplomats were recalled. Now they have returned, but it is impossible to know what future trends will be. Looking at pre-Cultural Revolution statistics, China ranks considerably below even other second-ranking powers in terms of number of diplomats abroad (see Table 6-17). China's diplomatic presence has improved considerably since the Cultural Revolution, but it still does not compare to other second-ranking powers. China's foreign missions are usually large, and this suggests a strong will to be a global power. However, China's success, as measured by its total presence abroad, suggests much less will, or constricted ambitions and frustrations.

The foregoing quantitative comparisons indicate that China's will is moderately high, but not outstanding. Clearly, China does not compete with the superpowers in strength of will and, although trends are difficult to measure, the available data do not indicate that China's determination to be a world power is increasing. One reason may be that Chinese leaders have received very little positive conditioning in the past two decades. Chinese leaders have been constrained from both military and

TABLE 6–17

DIPLOMATS SENT ABROAD BY LEADING NATIONS, 1964–1965

U.S.A.	2,782
U.K.	1,403
U.S.S.R.	1,345
France	1,152
W. Germany	671
Japan	638
U.A.R.	550
Italy	511
India	467
Czechoslovakia	442
Turkey	392
China	389
Canada	388
Poland	386
Netherlands	352
Indonesia	348
Spain	306
Argentina	301
Brazil	300

SOURCE: Chadwick F. Alger and Steven J. Brams, "Patterns of Representation in National Capitals and Intergovernmental Organizations," *World Politics*, 1967.

diplomatic adventures by the superpowers as well as neutral nations, and by world public opinion generally. The only positive reinforcement Chinese decision makers have received for changing the status quo is in helping the poor nations of the world (and here Chinese capabilities are meager) and China's in efforts to help revolutionary regimes and groups (which have largely been abandoned in an effort to attain greater formal influence in world affairs and to win U.S. support to balance the Soviet threat to China).

An analysis of the view that China is a nation with a strong will is in order, since the figures just presented do not confirm this observation. The fact that Mao's regime inspired Chinese nationalism has made it appear that China's desire to resume its place as a world power is very strong; and, though latent, it may be. But considering China's actions apart from pronouncements and threats, this has not been translated into the will to be a world power. Probably most telling is the fact that Peking allows part of what is generally regarded as its territory to remain as colonies in the hands of foreign powers. Hong Kong is administered by the United Kingdom, and Macao by Portugal. Taiwan remains in the hands of a competitive regime. China has made claim to vast amounts of territory that historically belonged to it. But only against India has it made any positive effort to get any of this land, and that action seemed to be more for strategic reasons than to get back territory based on irredentist claims. Peking has signed border agreements with all of the nations on its borders save India and the Soviet Union, and in no case can a good argument be made that China used force or pressure against these smaller nations for territorial gains. On the contrary, all, or almost all, of the settlements were to the benefit of the other country, and in most cases China, at least formally speaking, gave up part or all of its territorial claim.[28] Meanwhile, millions of overseas Chinese, especially in Southeast Asia, are neglected by Peking even when they are persecuted or discriminated against by local governments. Peking generally has taken the attitude that they are foreign citizens, even though they have been counted in China's census records.

Regarding its territorial integrity, China has also been slow to react to violations made by other countries. Since 1949 the United States has encroached upon China's territorial rights in a variety of ways. Spy planes were frequently sent over China, and reconnaissance ships entered China's waters.[29] For two and one-half decades, U.S. Navy ships patrolled the Taiwan Strait, often near the Nationalist-held islands of Quemoy and Matsu—just shouting distance from the Chinese mainland. During the Vietnam War, U.S. fighter planes frequently entered Chinese airspace, while U.S. aircraft carriers with atomic bombs on board docked in Hong Kong. Elsewhere, Soviet military incursions have been made into China, and dissenting minority groups have been enticed into the Soviet Union for military training. In few cases has the Chinese reaction gone beyond trying to stop incursions already in Chinese territory, or making some kind of verbal protest.

Finally, although Chinese leaders have made statements to the effect that they do not fear nuclear war and do not consider atomic weapons awesome or frightening, there is no real evidence that they really believe this.[30] Peking has sworn no-first-use, and has consistently refrained from making any threats with its nuclear weapons—quite in contrast to the United States and the Soviet Union.[31] China has not supplied nuclear weapons to any other country, and it is not known to have ever taken any atomic weapons outside of its own territory. There is no evidence to indicate that this policy will change.

Considering that China was demeaned and humiliated by the Western powers for more than a century, that China has not been able to play the important role in world affairs that historically belonged to it, and that in recent years both the United States and the Soviet Union have made direct efforts to deny China a more important world role, China's level of dissatisfaction should be high. And it is. Chinese leaders have shown the determination to contend against efforts to contain China and deny it a role in world politics. But China has done much less than most have anticipated. Moreover, its determination is usually expressed in quite indirect ways. In general, Peking has behaved cautiously, and has avoided direct confrontation with other countries, particularly the two superpowers.

In conclusion, it appears that China's totalitarian political system is clearly not the advantage that many analysts have argued. It is indeed questionable whether or not China has achieved a totalitarian system. It lacks an effective system of mass communication and some of the other requirements of social control that a totalitarian system should have. Also, the Chinese polity is still evolving, both in terms of the political system and its ideology. Thus, much remains uncertain. Because China is alienated from much of the world for ideological and other reasons, its political system cannot be considered an unqualified asset and, as international politics evolve toward greater concern for human rights and democracy, it may be a minus in terms of global influence. Expectations concerning China's diplomacy were overstated in the 1950s and early 1960s. Subsequently, there was considerable pessimism. Peking made important advances in the early 1970s, but at this point it is uncertain what advantages—in view of the Sino-Soviet dispute and the U.S.-Soviet detente—will accrue to China. China still has less global influence than it deserves, especially considering its population and resources, and it will doubtless increase its diplomatic influence in coming years. But as China starts to play a more important global role, it will face an increasing number of competitors. Third World countries will probably increase their international influence at a similar or faster rate. And the superpowers seem capable of maintaining special diplomatic influence. China's will has also been grossly overestimated, in part because of both fear and guilty conscience in the West as well as views that are based upon historical inevitabilities. Certainly, the facts do not portray Chinese leaders as being strong in will.

Looking at its strengths and weakness in these areas collectively, China must be regarded as a second-ranking power. It has some marked advantages over the other second-ranking powers, but it also has some outstanding handicaps. When averaging them out, China probably cannot be perceived to be clearly ahead or behind. And the same must be said about future prospects.

7

China's Scientific and Technological Capabilities

A cursory examination of China's status in science and technology gives the impression that China has made considerable progress in these areas in recent years but that the gap between China and its competitors for world-power status is still considerable. Put another way, China's backwardness in this general area is a major weakness in terms of its national strength and its international influence. On the other hand many perceive that China will experience rapid progress in the next decade or so and overcome this handicap. The major focus of analysis in this chapter, then, will be on the questions of how far China is behind competing powers and what its prospects are of catching up.

An optimistic view regarding China's prospects for progressive change in science and technology, at a rate making it possible to surpass its competitors in a few years, is based on the following: the history of scientific achievement in China, its favorable climate and large population, the ability of China to absorb quickly foreign scientific knowledge and technology virtually free of charge, the fact that China is now politically stable and its leaders desire to see scientific progress and can induce it, and the success of scientific and technological development since 1949.

Even a superficial study of history reveals that China has made contributions in science that overshadow most other nations. Many important inventions came from China: paper, the compass, gunpowder, printing, the mechanical clock, and the casting of iron. Prior to the Renaissance in Europe, the level of scientific knowledge and attainment in China far surpassed the rest of the world. Based upon this productive past, one can argue that recent centuries simply mark a temporary lull in China's greatness in this realm and that it will soon be reestablished. The fact that tremendous emphasis has been given to education and to scientific and technological research since 1949 seems to indicate that now is a time for resurgence. Also contributing to this view is the fact that China has made some novel, if not significant, discoveries or inventions in recent years: the first production of synthetic insulin, artificial benzene, and a machine for growing silicon crystals.

Another line of argument for China's potential growth in science is that China lies geographically in latitudes or climatic zones where scientific attainment has been almost a monopoly and that, since geniuses generally represent a small but constant portion of the population in any nation, China has more geniuses because it has more people. Clearly, empirical evidence shows that intellectual accomplishment as well as scientific progress has occurred mainly, almost exclusively, in climatic zones similar to China's. It is also true that creative or scientific minds, or even intelligent people, tend to comprise a rather small but generally representative body of most populations. China naturally has more of them.

A third theoretical argument that China can and will develop rapidly in science and technology is that scientific knowledge is generally a free commodity, like the air; and since China has a well-developed educational tradition, it can absorb what it needs from abroad—quickly, easily, and with little or no expense. The fact that technological diffusion has been much more rapid in recent years, and the time lag for new technology to take root in other nations or environments has been shortened, is offered as further proof of this view. And there seems to be real evidence to prove this thesis: in the first years of Communist rule, the Chinese government obtained large quantities of books, data, etc. from the Soviet Union that were put into immediate use in upgrading China's technological and scientific information. By 1957 some 12,400 Russian books had been translated and published in China.[1] In this way China avoided a large amount of time-consuming and expensive research and experimentation. There seems to be no reason why this cannot continue.

A less theoretical and probably more potent argument for China's prospects in science and technology is that the present regime has provided the proper milieu for progress in learning, both in terms of affording political and social stability and in supplying the impetus or goal-orientation for progress in education as well as in science and technology. The government has expended tremendous efforts to eradicate illiteracy, has restructured education based upon centralized planning and control, and has forced specialization and concentration in scientific courses of study as opposed to less practical curricula (see Tables 7−1 and 7−2). Finally, there are now no private institutions of higher learning in China; the subjects taught in all schools are determined by the state, and students are directed into fields of study to fit their aptitudes rather than their interests. Thus, specific goals can be pursued in unity and nationwide.

Commensurate with this "revolution" in education, in 1949 and after, more money was provided for science and research. State allocations for education and for science increased severalfold just a few years after the Communists took over China (see Table 7−3). In one year alone, 1956, the budget for science under the headings Culture, Education, and Health increased from $15 million to just under $100 million.[2] Similar increases were made in following years to provide buildings and new research institutes, and to buy books, journals, records, and equipment from abroad.

Other facts can be cited to augment the argument that the progress made in education, science, and technology since 1949 is evidence that

TABLE 7−1

HIGHER EDUCATION ENROLLMENT, 1948−1960

School Year	Entrants	Enrollment	Graduates
1948–49	−*	−	21,000
1949–50	−	117,000	18,000
1950–51	35,000	137,000	19,000
1951–52	35,000	153,000	32,000
1952–53	65,900	191,000	48,000
1953–54	71,400	212,000	47,000
1954–55	94,000	253,000	53,000
1955–56	96,200	288,000	63,000
1956–57	165,600	403,000	56,000
1957–58	107,000	441,000	72,000
1958–59	152,000	660,000	62,200
1959–60	270,000	810,000	−

SOURCE: Immanuel C. Y. Hsu, "Higher Education in Communist China, 1949−61," in Roderick MacFarquhar, ed., *China Under Mao: Politics Takes Command* (Cambridge, Mass.: Massachusetts Institute of Technology Press, 1966).

*Dash indicates information not available.

TABLE 7–2

HIGHER EDUCATION ENROLLMENT BY FIELD, 1928–1958

(percent)

School Year	Engineering	Science	Agriculture and Forestry	Health	Political Science and Law	Education	Finance and Economics	Literature and Arts	Total
1928–32	10.2%	8.3%	3.8%	4.0%	38.2%	7.8%	5.9%	21.8%	100.0%
1933–37	14.4	12.8	4.9	10.5	23.5	8.1	6.9	18.9	100.0
1938–42	21.0	11.3	7.3	8.6	20.2	9.8	10.4	11.4	100.0
1943–47	18.6	7.3	7.2	8.0	22.1	13.6	11.6	11.6	100.0
1949–50	26.0	6.0	8.9	13.0	6.3	10.6	16.7	12.5	100.0
1950–51	27.8	—*	—	12.5	—	9.6	—	—	49.9
1951–52	31.2	—	—	13.8	—	11.7	—	—	56.7
1952–53	34.8	5.0	8.1	12.9	2.0	16.7	11.5	9.0	100.0
1953–54	37.7	5.8	7.2	13.7	1.8	19.4	6.4	8.0	100.0
1954–55	37.5	6.8	6.3	13.4	1.6	21.8	4.4	8.2	100.0
1955–56	38.1	6.9	7.5	12.7	1.7	21.9	3.9	7.3	100.0
1956–57	36.8	6.3	—	—	—	24.3	—	—	67.4
1957–58	40.9	6.2	8.6	12.6	2.1	21.3	2.9	5.4	100.0

SOURCE: Immanuel C. Y. Hsu, "Higher Education in Communist China, 1949–61," in MacFarquhar, ed., *China Under Mao: Politics Takes Command* (Cambridge, Mass.: Massachusetts Institute of Technology Press, 1966).

*Dash indicates information not available, therefore figures for these years do not total 100 percent.

TABLE 7–3

Science Budget in China, 1950–1960

Year	Total Budget (U.S. dollars)	Percent of National Budget
1950	$ 408,000	0.015%
1951	3,212,000	0.07
1952	4,628,000	0.07
1953	13,000,000	0.15
1954	13,836,000	0.14
1955	15,410,000	0.14
1956	99,590,000	0.80
1957	119,600,000	1.00
1958	156,734,000	0.90
1959	334,700,000	1.57
1960	441,224,000	1.54

Source: John M. H. Lindbeck, "The Organization and Development of Science," in MacFarquhar, ed., *China Under Mao: Politics Takes Command* (Cambridge, Mass.: Massachusetts Institute of Technology Press, 1966).

efforts by the regime to create a new learning environment unencumbered by the past have been successful. Whereas prior to 1949 only about 15 percent of the Chinese population was literate and only a small fraction attended school, almost everyone is now literate to the degree of reading newspapers.[3] By 1958 the following increases in school enrollment in China were attained: primary schools, 164 percent; junior middle schools, 483 percent; senior middle schools, 303 percent; and high schools and colleges, 277 percent.[4] By 1961 China was producing graduate engineers in numbers equal to 75 percent of those coming out of U.S. colleges and universities, and the rate of annual increase was much larger.[5] In addition, Chinese education and science were linked directly to industrial production and specific projects that would increase national strength.

Underscoring its scientific accomplishments, in 1964 China exploded its first nuclear device, after which it continued to develop bigger and more sophisticated weapons. China tested missile delivery systems and, in 1970, launched a man-made satellite that had a more circular orbit than those first put into space by either the Soviet Union or the United States.

Looking now at the counterarguments, the belief that because China was a historical giant in science and education it therefore can play such a role again is based upon a theory of historical inevitability that has doubtful validity when applied to any area, but especially to scientific achievement. Most of the other ancient civilizations that provided the world with intellectual accomplishments—Egypt, Greece, India, Peru, Phoenicia, Rome—have had no resurgence and have demonstrated no special proclivity in scientific achievement based upon their past greatness. On the contrary, most of the countries that are now scientifically advanced have little or no ancient tradition in science; thus, one might make the same argument in reverse.

The position that China is favored with a suitable climate may be true, but probably is not as important as it might be when considering the air-conditioning revolution. It also must be remembered that, with the exception of India, China is not competing for world-power status with any nation in an unfavorable climatic zone. The other part of the argument—that the number of geniuses tends to be constant, therefore China should have more—is overshadowed by the importance of money, the application of science to production, and the need for goal orientation in research. Without money, research cannot be undertaken; and without an application, the likelihood of its being continued is small. Also, scientific research is usually meaningless if it is not directed toward certain well-planned goals. These factors seem to be much more important in forecasting a nation's progress in science and technology than the number of intelligent people in the nation. As we will see later, China is seriously handicapped in all these areas. China's progress since 1949 was from a very low base, and China remains far behind the other powers, except India, in the number of scientists and technicians as a percentage of the population (see Table 7–4).

The argument that knowledge is a free commodity that crosses national borders like the wind is greatly exaggerated and applies much

TABLE 7–4

SCIENTISTS IN RESEARCH AND DEVELOPMENT IN SELECTED NATIONS
(percent per 10,000 population)

U.S.A.	26.0%
U.S.S.R.	18.0
U.K.	13.0
Japan	11.7
France	11.5
W. Germany	11.2
Canada	11.0
China	1.0
India	0.7

SOURCE: *Federal Policy, Plans and Organization for Science and Technology*, Part II (Washington, D.C.: U.S. Government Printing Office, 1974).

better to the recent past than to the present. Moreover, it applies best to special or unique situations and conditions that are not present in China. The most rapid technology spread has occurred among the developed capitalist countries, and this is still true. Joint business agreements and multinational corporations provide an important conduit for technology transfer. Governments also purchase technology from or through other governments but, with few exceptions, this occurs only among friendly or allied governments. In many cases, technology transfer has appeared "free" because of military or political alliances or alliance systems. This certainly describes the situation whereby Japan attained massive amounts of patents, formulas, and manufacturing techniques from the United States during the 1950s and 1960s. The same was true of China's relationship with the Soviet Union in the first decade after 1949. China was able to obtain technology from the Soviet Union free, or at a very low cost, because of their military alliance. However, the situation is now very different.

Today a lead in technology may enable one nation to corner the market on a product so quickly that other nations that try to develop or make operational a new technology are handicapped because they cannot break into the market or it is already saturated. Also, in most nations more and more advanced technology involves government contracts or controls and is therefore classified. Penalties are meted out for sale or other transfer. Large global corporations also maintain control over much technology that is used to production, and they share it only with countries wherein they have operations—generally not including China.

The argument that the present government has broken down or destroyed traditional or cultural impediments that prevented China from developing scientifically during the last several centuries and has provided a favorable climate for educational and scientific progress can also be doubted. In eradicating cultural obstacles to science, it appears that some have been done away with, but others remain. And, in some ways, new blocks replace old ones. Clearly, Peking's anti-capitalist, anti-imperialist ideology was a handicap to China's quest for scientific and technological progress in the 1950s. It prompted China to rely exclusively upon the Soviet Union for books, models, and techniques while eschewing anything from Western countries. Since inherent in the Soviet model are features that lead to uneven development in science and technology, China inherited this problem. Even more unpropitious to China was the fact that it became dependent upon the Soviet Union, and when the break with the Kremlin occurred in 1960, its only meaningful source of books, technology, and other aids was severed. This caused a severe setback, the magnitude of which can be seen in the fact that in one month 1,390 Soviet scientists left China and 343 project contracts were torn up.[6] As a result, China's scientific development was delayed five to ten years.

Although China is now buying large amounts of technology from Western countries, Chinese attitudes are frequently an obstacle to efficiency in both obtaining and using foreign techniques and knowledge. For example, when China purchased jet engines from the United Kingdom in 1964, technicians and advisors were included in the contract; but they were used infrequently and only when the Chinese encountered difficulties. They could have been employed to shorten the skill acquisition process and to set up repair facilities, but were not.[7] China's cautiousness toward foreign countries also motivates it to seek many different sources of technology, which makes repair and improvement or alteration extremely complicated. Another problem is that without proper advice and consultation China frequently copies Western techniques and machines that were unsuccessful, or obsolete by the time of China's acquisition.[8]

Related to this problem is the slow progress made in China in language reform. The Chinese language is very difficult and time-consuming to acquire and does not lend itself to learning in the sciences. Peking has set forth various decrees regarding language reform, and has started various movements and campaigns to change the language. Many Chinese characters have been simplified, and the vernacular is now used in most newspapers and books in China. Still, Chinese nationalism seems to ensure that the language will not be romanized, since this would destroy much of Chinese history.[9] And despite simplification, Chinese is not conducive to effective scientific writing, is extremely cumbersome to adapt to the computer, and does not translate easily. The translation problem is further compounded by the fact that in the 1950s everything was geared to Russian, and after the split China had to rely upon other languages for importing technology and lacked skilled translaters. Currently, Peking's policy of self-reliance forces Chinese scientists to learn several foreign languages, which is unduly time-consuming.

While the Communists have been successful in altering the style of learning that previously emphasized language and the arts, doctrinaire ideology has interfered with the growth of objectivity and secular attitudes in some ways unprecedented in Chinese history. The fact that Party ideologues have decision-making authority over the allocation of money in education and research, and that they are able to dictate the precedence of projects, assign research personnel, and even promote and demote without regard to professional competence, has had a serious negative influence on progress in science and technology in China.[10] The party also has engineered numerous purges in the scientific community. The first large-scale purge followed the Hundred Flowers Campaign in 1956, when scholars and scientists criticized the party for its arrogance, class-consciousness, and arbitrariness, and its meddling in education and research. In retaliation, the party cut funds for higher education and research, and punished many scientists. This was repeated on a much broader scale during the Cultural Revolution: colleges were closed, research institutes torn apart, and scientists ridiculed or sent to farms to perform manual labor. In 1967 alone, 3,000 members of the Academy of Sciences, China's most prestigious scientific institution, were sent to the countryside.[11] During the period as a whole nearly half of China's scientists were in some way punished.[12] And the movement was not short-lived in its effects; from the onset of the movement in 1966 to 1972, almost no students graduated from institutions of higher learning. Measured against 1964, when the Cultural Revolution was launched, by 1975 (six years after the Cultural Revolution ended), enrollments in institutions of higher learning in China were down 4.4 percent.[13] Sixty magazines stopped publication during this period and have not since reappeared. Specialized industries—such as the transistor industry, which was associated with the purged head-of-state Liu Shao-ch'i—bore the brunt of criticism and attack for more than five years.[14]

Against this background, we can now examine the contributions made to education by the present government and try to assess its significance in terms of making China a powerful nation. In the area of mass education, Chinese leaders have achieved what are generally regarded as very impressive accomplishments. The literacy rate in China has improved from about 15 percent prior to 1949 to somewhere between 40 and 80 percent by 1970, depending upon one's definition of literacy. This will certainly continue to facilitate the industrialization process and help economic development in some important ways. On the other hand, the literacy rate in China, using Western standards in defining the term, is still far below all of the nations with which it will compete for world power status, except India (see Table 7−5). In coming years, China un-

TABLE 7-5

PERCENT OF LITERATE POPULATION IN SELECTED NATIONS

France	100.0%
Japan	100.0
U.K.	100.0
W. Germany	99.9
U.S.S.R.	99.7
U.S.A.	99.0
Canada	94.8
China	40.0
India	29.4

SOURCE: *Encyclopedia Britannica,* 1975.

doubtedly will close the gap (as will India), but it is doubtful that this will occur in the next decade or two.

Chinese leaders have also greatly enlarged the number of China's elementary and middle schools, which, when combined with half-work, half-study classes, provide education to almost all of the young people in China. It undoubtedly is here that China has made the most laudable progress in the past three decades. Nevertheless, the quality of education given and the appropriateness of the learning can be questioned. A considerable amount of the study at this level amounts to little more than eradicating illiteracy. It must also be realized that one of the goals of education in China, in addition to serving as a socialization process, is to control idleness and unemployment, and for this reason perhaps less should be expected. Thus, the value of primary education in China in terms of producing scientists and technicians is not high. Although it is difficult to judge the quality of lower education in China compared with other countries, it is clear that the facilities and teacher training are less adequate and that this would be at least somewhat true of the general quality of education at this level. One objective standard for comparison is the teacher-student ratio, which is clearly less favorable in China than in other competing nations (see Table 7-6).

Unlike basic education, higher education has obviously not fared well due to the stress placed on equality and the antagonisms between the regime and the intelligentsia. In spite of its population advantage, China ranks only fifth among the major powers in the number of students in higher education, and places last, even below India, in terms of the number of students per capita in institutions of higher learning (see Tables 7-7 and 7-8). This certainly does not bode well for building a large

TABLE 7−6

Student-Teacher Ratio in Primary and Secondary Schools in Selected Nations

	Number of Students per Teacher	
	Primary	Secondary
France	23.0	—
Japan	25.8	12.0
U.K.	26.8	17.3
U.S.A.	28.1	14.8
W. Germany	32.1	21.6
China	33.0	25.0
India	38.0	28.5

SOURCE: *Encyclopedia Britannica,* 1975.

TABLE 7−7

Full-time Students in Higher Education in Selected Nations

U.S.A.	9,023,466
U.S.S.R.	4,751,100
India	2,540,000
Japan	2,087,866
China	820,000
France	763,980
W. Germany	729,207
Canada	592,000
U.K.	397,621

SOURCE: *Encyclopedia Britannica 1977 Book of the Year.*

TABLE 7−8

Number of College Graduates in Selected Nations
(per 10,000 population)

U.S.A.	544
Japan	333
Canada	329
France	321
U.S.S.R.	235
W. Germany	139
India	52
China	33

SOURCE: *Encyclopedia Britannica,* 1975.

scientific community, capable of competing with the major powers, since it is almost exclusively higher education that provides the necessary talent for scientific and technological progress.

The amount of money spent on education by China and other major world powers is similarly revealing. When China's educational system is taken as a whole, its expenditures rank it ninth among the top nations of the world behind nations such as Canada and Italy, which normally are not thought of as serious contenders for world power status (see Table 7–9).

In terms of the proportion of gross national product spent on education, China ranks even lower. It spends 3.7 percent of its GNP on education, giving it a rank of 53rd in the world.[15] This is reflective of lack of funds, but also seems to suggest a lack of determination on the part of the Chinese government. It also says something about the quality, and ultimately the productiveness, of China's intellectuals.

A like situation prevails in scientific research. China's expenditures on research and development give China a rank of eighth among the major powers, ahead of only India (see Table 7–10). Japan spends more than six times the amount China spends on research and development, while the United States tops China's budget by more than 65-fold. China's ranking is the same when the percent of GNP devoted to research and development is considered—suggesting that the regime is not as committed to science to the degree that many of its pronouncements suggest or as much as other competing nations (see Table 7–11).

It is difficult to be sure what criteria or standards should be used to

TABLE 7–9

EDUCATION EXPENDITURES BY LEADING POWERS, 1965
(million U.S. dollars)

U.S.A.	$36,687
U.S.S.R.	22,849
U.K.	5,094
Japan	4,111
W. Germany	3,832
France	3,439
Italy	3,112
Canada	3,039
China	2,800
India	1,002

SOURCE: *World-Wide Military Expenditures and Related Data* (Washington, D.C.: U.S. Arms Control and Disarmament Agency, 1965).

TABLE 7–10

RESEARCH AND DEVELOPMENT EXPENDITURES BY SELECTED NATIONS, 1969
(million U.S. dollars)

U.S.A.	$2,748.62
U.S.S.R.	828.00
Japan	267.52
France	265.24
W. Germany	260.61
U.K.	251.62
Canada	103.05
China	41.50
India	14.40

SOURCE: *Federal Policy, Plans and Organization for Science and Technology,* Part II (Washington, D.C., 1974).

TABLE 7–11

RESEARCH AND DEVELOPMENT EXPENDITURES AS PERCENTAGE OF
GROSS NATIONAL PRODUCT IN SELECTED NATIONS

U.S.A.	2.9%
U.S.S.R.	2.3
U.K.	2.3
France	1.9
W. Germany	1.7
Japan	1.6
Canada	1.5
China	0.5
India	0.3

SOURCE: *Federal Policy, Plans and Organization for Science and Technology,* Part II (Washington, D.C., 1974).

rate nations in their scientific development other than those already mentioned, which focus on the educational system and research and development personnel and budgets. However, two areas that are frequently cited as evidence of China's scientific accomplishments are nuclear weapons and advanced delivery systems. China's ranking in these areas was discussed in chapter 5. Reiterating for a moment, it was noted that there is a tremendous gap between China and the two superpowers in both areas. In terms of nuclear weapons development, China probably still ranks behind France and the United Kingdom, but it is close to them and may be catching up. In delivery systems, it has a similar ranking, but does not have the related technological capabilities possessed by France and the United Kingdom—a factor which may influence future progress.

Moreover, some of China's competitors for world-power status, such as Japan and West Germany, are not actively competing in nuclear and missile technology. Others, such as Canada, India, and the United Kingdom, do not seek national independence in terms of nuclear technology. Thus, an assessment of weapons development probably does not present a fair basis for comparison of the scientific capabilities of China's competitors. In terms of the development of nuclear power for peaceful uses, China is behind a number of other countries, although this is partly because China has more than sufficient alternative forms of energy.

In space technology, as reflected in the launching of earth satellites, China ranks sixth. It is behind both superpowers in terms of the number of launchings of satellites by more than 100 times, and trails France, Italy, and Japan (see Table 7–12). West Germany has not seriously entered the field because it is able to utilize U.S. facilities. Also it would constitute a duplication of effort, since other European Common Market countries, notably France and Italy, have programs that are shared. The same reasons also explain the United Kingdom's rank. China may be able to make some gains vis-à-vis individual European nations in coming years, but it will be virtually impossible to close the gap between it and the superpowers in the near future, and it is unlikely that it will be able to compete with the European Community as a group.

In the area of computers, which many scientists argue is a reliable basis for predicting future scientific progress because of the need to collect, store, and manipulate large amounts of data, China is so far behind that it is not even cited among the leading nations in possession of large computers (see Table 7–13). The United States has such a lead in this

TABLE 7–12

SUCCESSFUL EARTH SATELLITE LAUNCHINGS

	Total Launchings (through 1975)	Initial Launching
U.S.S.R.	878	1957
U.S.A.	645	1958
France	10	1965
Italy	8	1967
Japan	7	1970
China	5	1970
Australia	1	1967
U.K.	1	1970

SOURCE: *Aeronautics and Space Report of the President, 1975* (Washington, D.C.: NASA, 1976).

TABLE 7–13

LEADING NATIONS BY NUMBER OF LARGE COMPUTERS

U.S.A.	70,000
Japan	5,800
W. Germany	5,750
U.K.	5,600
France	5,010
U.S.S.R.	3,500
Italy	2,500
Canada	2,400
Australia	900
Netherlands	850
Switzerland	800

SOURCE: Zbigniew Brzezinski, "America and Europe," *Foreign Affairs*, October 1970.

area that it may be said to possess a monopoly. For this reason, most other Western nations have tied their computer development to U.S. companies through joint programs or subsidiary companies. So far this has proved to be a workable and efficient arrangement. Even the Soviet Union has sought to obtain computer technology from the United States. China has also, but Peking is reluctant to make any deals with the United States beyond buying large computers or computer systems. It is trying to develop computer technology on its own, and although it has the advantage of considerable progress in semiconductor technology, it seems hopeless for China to try to develop competitive capabilities due to its late start, the high cost of research, and the difficulties in adapting the Chinese language to computers.

The authorship of scientific articles, monographs, and books and the publication of scientific journals is another benchmark of a nation's scientific accomplishment or the standards of attainment in that country. In both respects, China ranks very low; in fact, it is not competitive with any of the other second-ranking powers. In scientific authorship, China ranks 47th of all nations in the world, while its contributions are only a small fraction of those of any competitive power (see Table 7–14). In the publication of scientific journals, China ties with Holland for thirteenth ranking in the world (see Table 7–15). Nor does China rank among the top ten nations in recipients of Nobel prizes or in the number of technological innovations.[16] Although the data listed on both of these tables is somewhat old, more recent surveys show a similar or worse situation for China. During the Cultural Revolution, China's scientific research declined in both quantity and quality, and in relative terms China probably has not

TABLE 7-14

LEADING NATIONS BY CONTRIBUTION TO SCIENTIFIC AUTHORSHIP, 1961
(percent of world's total)

1.	U.S.A.	41.7000	25.	Spain	0.2600
2.	U.K.	10.1700	26.	Argentina	0.2400
3.	U.S.S.R.	8.2000	27.	Yugoslavia	0.2300
4.	W. Germany	6.8900	28.	New Zealand	0.2300
5.	France	5.4400	29.	United Arab	
6.	Japan	4.2200		Republic	0.2100
7.	Canada	3.3700	30.	Brazil	0.1600
8.	India	2.2600	31.	Ireland	0.1300
9.	Italy	1.9800	32.	Greece	0.1100
10.	Australia	1.8000	33.	Mexico	0.1100
11.	Switzerland	1.3500	34.	Chile	0.0960
12.	Czechoslovakia	1.2900	35.	Nigeria	0.0740
13.	Sweden	1.2800	36.	Venezuela	0.0610
14.	Poland	0.9500	37.	Taiwan	0.0580
15.	Israel	0.8600	38.	Pakistan	0.0550
16.	Hungary	0.7600	39.	Turkey	0.0450
17.	Belgium	0.7300	40.	Lebanon	0.0430
18.	Denmark	0.5700	41.	Iran	0.0430
19.	Australia	0.5300	42.	Jamaica	0.0370
20.	Romania	0.4400	43.	Portugal	0.0370
21.	Norway	0.3700	44.	Thailand	0.0330
22.	Finland	0.3600	45.	Kenya	0.0320
23.	Bulgaria	0.2700	46.	Hong Kong	0.0300
24.	S. Africa	0.2600	47.	China	0.0290

SOURCE: Charles L. Taylor and Michael C. Hudson, *World Handbook of Political and Social Indicators*, (New Haven: Yale University Press, 1972).

TABLE 7-15

LEADING NATIONS IN PUBLICATION OF SIGNIFICANT SCIENTIFIC JOURNALS

1.	U.S.A.	6,000
2.	Japan	2,820
3.	France	2,780
4.	W. Germany	2,560
5.	U.S.S.R.	2,100
6.	U.K.	2,090
7.	Italy	1,530
8.	Belgium	1,260
9.	Switzerland	810
10.	Poland	750
11.	Sweden	710
12.	India	670
13.	China	660
13.	Holland	660
14.	Brazil	650

SOURCE: Charles M. Gottschalk and Winifred F. Desmond, "World-Wide Census of Scientific and Technical Serials," *American Documentation*, (Washington, D.C., 1963).

regained its former rank. According to one recent study, for example, China was not among the top fifteen nations in scientific publications during the period 1965–1973.[17] And in 1975 China was not listed among the top ten in publishing in any of the following specific scientific fields: molecular biology, systematic biology, chemistry, earth sciences, engineering, mathematics, clinical medicine, physics, psychology, and space sciences.[18]

Examining in greater depth the obstacles that China faces in improving its science and technology may make possible further conclusions concerning China's future strengths and weaknesses in these areas. It also will make it easier to judge the magnitude of China's lag in these realms and to predict whether or not significant progress can be attained so that eventually this lag will not be a handicap to world-power status.

One major problem is that China lacks a pattern for the application of technology. During the initial years of Communist rule, the Soviet Union served as a model. China sought to develop heavy industry as an infrastructure, not only for economic development but also as the basis for technological and scientific development. The directing of technology and science toward the industrialization process, which the Chinese called the "mobilization model," fostered various kinds of problems and eventually was scrapped. In some critical ways the model was not appropriate for China since China could not afford the investment that the Soviet Union allocated to heavy industry and did not have the raw materials available at the time to generate rapid growth in the industrial sector.[19] Moreover, food production in China could not be neglected as it had been in the Soviet Union during the initial period of industrialization. Finally, China did not have the funds to spend on science and technology that the Soviet Union had. Even though by 1957 Peking allocated a record figure of between $400 and $500 million to science annually, this still represented only about one-tenth of what Moscow had in its budget that year.

Another problem with adopting the Soviet model was that relations between China and the Soviet Union turned sour in the late 1950s, and when this happened it became evident that China had placed too much reliance upon the Kremlin. The break not only caused a tremendous backsliding in scientific research, but also disillusioned many Chinese scientists. Understandably, it forced the Chinese leadership to disconnect research from the industrial process. This allowed scientists to pursue research simply for the sake of research, which, for the most part, ended up being work that led to nothing or was duplicated elsewhere.[20] As a compromise solution, China took to importing machinery and equipment from the West, but without acquiring the know-how required for application; so again, there was considerable waste and inefficiency.

The alternative—the capitalist design—is no doubt unsuitable to China in view of the commitment of the regime to maintain economic equality and its use of the Communist political model. Even if Peking were to make the decision to change to the capitalist model (which is not being suggested), it would be difficult and would take considerable time. A major problem would be gearing the country to using technology in the production of consumer goods while linking this production to foreign trade. It would also take time for Chinese goods to gain acceptance in the Western business community. At present, as a Communist country China does not obtain any of the benefits of bloc membership in terms of information exchange or sources of technology, and it is regarded with caution by the Western business community despite the attractiveness of the Chinese market.

A second problem, and one resulting in part from the first, is that scientific research and technology usage in China are not organized in terms of objectives. In other words, there is inadequate leadership and direction given to scientific work, in spite of what is purported to be complete party control over education and research. The stated purpose of investment in science and technology, as is true of higher education, is to strengthen the nation and facilitate modernization. The party defines more specifically what this means, but often in contradictory or confusing ways. And in so doing, it comes to loggerheads with scientists and researchers.[21] This has evoked the "red versus expert" controversy discussed earlier in two other contexts. This problem is very acute in the scientific community and in higher education, and characterizes the party's relationship with intellectuals. One way to avoid this problem might be to assign to the military the task, or at least part of the task, of giving goal-orientation to much scientific work, as is done in the United States and in the Soviet Union. In China, however, the military is not suited to this role. Also, the demands of the military for funds constitute a special problem for the party, and for this reason party leaders are reluctant to give the military greater prerogatives that might increase its appetite for money. Hence, scientific research and utilization of the products of science and technology involve a serious lack of coordination. In short, China lacks a map for guiding scientific research to a final end.

Intimately related to this problem is the fact that scientific and technological progress in China is very uneven. In some areas, China is quite advanced and can even compare with, or compete with, most other second-ranking powers. In others, it is far behind and would have to be categorized as backward or underdeveloped. Due to this situation, there is little spread effect of technology in China. This is partly the product of giving high priority and the allocation of an inordinate amount of funds to certain projects, such as nuclear weapons, while sacrificing in other areas. However, it is also a result of a gap between science and management, the dispersion of industry for defense reasons, and inefficient transportation and communication systems.[22] Better planning may help to overcome this problem, but considerable time will be required, even if long-range national plans could be agreed upon and implemented.

Considering these difficulties, together with China's inability to devote much more money to education and science, the reasonable solution is to import more technology. In and of itself, this does not constitute a serious problem, since it is done by the other second-ranking powers and even by the Soviet Union. But real questions arise: how do China's absorptive capacities and its abilities to utilize imported technology compare to those of other competing powers? And what about China's attitudes and the willingness of other countries to cooperate with China or sell or give it technology?

China's absorptive capacity appears to be considerably less than that of competing powers, even India, because of the slower development of higher education in China. Another serious impediment is the relatively small number of skilled workers in China. Chinese attitudes also present an obstacle. Party cadres are jealous of their prerogatives and are unwilling to turn over decision-making authority to educational or scientific institutions. The fact that requirements in universities and technical institutes have been lowered to accommodate those with lesser intellectual backgrounds and inferior aptitudes may alleviate this problem, but it also reduces the quality of these institutions. China is also xenophobic regarding foreign technology, and relying upon foreign techniques entails the danger of fostering an inferiority complex on a mass scale. It is probably for this reason that to date China's technology imports have been primarily in the area of manufacturing while Peking eschews foreign design and management technology.[23]

Most other developing countries are not reluctant to import technology on a broad scale and are even willing to pay for foreign technicians.

Also, they allow foreign companies to establish themselves within their borders. In recent years, this has proved to be a very easy and effective means of technological acquisition. Many less developed countries market their labor to foreign companies, especially the big multinationals, while obtaining free technical or skill training. Many also specialize in order to sell in the developed countries' markets and finance additional projects. Some trade their resources for technology and technical training. All of these approaches are proven short cuts to scientific and technological progress, but Peking rejects and probably will continue to reject all or most of them.

Related to this is China's ability to pay for importing massive amounts of foreign technology. Until recently, China was free of debt and, in spite of heavy borrowing in the past few years, its credit rating remains excellent. However, Peking may be unwilling to go further into debt to pay for more know-how, technology, and plants. In any case, borrowing has its limits, and over the long run is not an adequate solution. Most other countries have financed long-term technology imports by specializing in certain consumer goods that could be put on the world market or sold in the country where more technology can be purchased. Japan is a classic case of success in using this formula. China is now doing this to some extent in the exploitation and sale of its oil. It has not done much in other areas though. And due to its lack of concern with consumerism, its fear of foreign influence, and its lack of internal transport facilities as well as adequate harbors and other foreign trade facilities, this does not hold a great deal of promise as a course of action for China. In any case, China would be in the game late; many other nations have followed the Japanese model to the point that the markets of the advanced nations are being flooded, and the potential for more extensive international trade, although still considerable, seems to be subject to bottlenecks and perhaps even limits to growth.

Thus, there is no breakthrough in sight for China. Its present policies cannot make China competitive in a world of growing specialization, where advances in science and technology owe so much to the freedom to do research without respect to government policies or social equality, where money must often be invested in what appear to be impractical ventures, and where cooperation with foreign scientists is so important. Its problems and backwardness in science and technology can be seen only as serious sources of weakness for China in the near future. Even in comparison with the underdeveloped world, China's potential cannot be viewed optimistically. Its inability and unwillingness to specialize and integrate its efforts with other nations constitute an obstacle that smaller and less-developed countries do not experience. China has some assets that most Third World countries do not have, but it is uncertain what role they will play in the future and whether or not they can compensate for the handicaps just mentioned. Compared to competing second-ranking powers and the superpowers, China is far behind, and it appears unlikely that it will close the gap in the near future. Clearly, its deficiencies in this ingredient of national power afford a serious impediment to world-power status in the future.

8

Summary and Conclusions

Although China possesses important assets that enable it to be a major actor in world politics, it is also handicapped by problems or liabilities in every category of national power. Moreover, compared to the superpowers, China demonstrates marked general weaknesses in every realm. Clearly, China is not a superpower and will not be in the future; China must be regarded as a second-ranking power. And China's rank among the second-ranking powers is not necessarily at the top. Reasons for this have already been cited. For the purposes of drawing conclusions concerning China's future role in global politics, it is relevant to examine China's overall capabilities in terms of strengths and weaknesses and relate these to the present requirements of international politics as well as to the nature of the evolving international system. The important questions are: What are China's assets and liabilities, and how will these affect the impact China will make as a new actor in international politics? What are Peking's specific roles in the global political arena? Where does China belong in the future hierarchy of world powers?

In terms of relative strengths and weaknesses, China may be considered better endowed in categories 1 and 2—geography and population, and natural resources. In categories 3 and 6—industrial and economic development, and science and technology—China is clearly weak. In categories 4 and 5—military strength, and political stability, diplomacy, and will—a definitive conclusion is more difficult. Since the present importance of each of these categories or ingredients of power is not the same, some kind of balance sheet must be drawn. Also, since the weight of each has changed since the concept of ingredients of power was first used, the importance of each, and hence China's overall strength as an international actor, can be projected into the future by examining trends in each area.

In the past, geographic size and population were considered the most important elements of power, and when scales were drawn or relative numbers assigned, these two, or the combination, generally received the greatest weight or score. The importance of manpower in building armies and the crucial role of natural boundaries or vast space, both of which served as barriers to attacking armies, made this so. In assessing the size factor, little attention was given to the fact that nations might be too large, and thus political control difficult or impossible, because such nations were either ethnically heterogeneous or undeveloped and these factors were considered the causes for their weakness. Likewise, there was no such thing as an overpopulation problem known to power analysts in the past. This remained generally true up to the end of World War II.

Although China is benefited by its large size and population, these two assets are not as important as they once were. And there are corollary liabilities involved. Feeding China's large population adequately is difficult. At the same time, agriculture is the main source of capital for investment in industrial development, and a high birth rate reduces agricultural surpluses. Certainly, further increases in population will not augment China's power status. In fact, overpopulation constitutes a serious weakness for China because of the need to generate capital from agriculture and the need to import food from the West. Thus, China's large population has to be considered a debit in the power equation as well as an asset. Future population increase must be seen as a liability. Population growth will be of benefit to those countries that are underpopulated and handicapped by a lack of population, but not to China. Australia, Brazil, and Canada are countries that will improve their power positions with an increase in their populations. Population increases may enhance somewhat the power of most other second-ranking or potential second-ranking powers, but this depends upon economic growth and a variety of other factors. The same applies to the Soviet Union and the United States. Therefore, assuming a future world population based upon current projections, China's relative power will decline.

Geographical barriers are not as important as they once were because psychological and economic warfare ignore national boundaries, defensible or otherwise, and sophisticated delivery systems carrying weapons of mass destruction cancel the importance of national armies built to protect the state.[1] Anyway, China does not possess natural or defensible frontiers, except for the mountains between China and India. China's geopolitical location is likewise a questionable asset. It might be important were China a superpower, but this is not the case. Its location and its lack of natural frontiers are costly in terms of its defense requirements.

In summary, then, China can be said to possess certain assets based upon its large population size and its geography. But it also possesses serious liabilities in both areas. Furthermore, China's assets in this realm have less application to the current world power balance than they had in the past and will be of decreasing importance in the future.

The possession of natural resources was considered an essential asset in the past because the development of industry was tied to the availability of resources. In the last century, all of the nations that became major powers did so based upon their industrial development—made possible by ready sources of raw materials. Coal and iron ore were considered the most crucial since they were the most vital to heavy industry. Subsequently, petroleum was added to the list. World War II confirmed the important role of raw materials in measuring national power, since the losing side suffered serious liabilities in this area which clearly led to its defeat. In the last few years the rapidly diminishing sources of raw materials and energy on a global scale, coupled with a marked increase in prices, have accentuated the importance of raw materials as an indicator of national power.

However, from the end of World War II until the recent oil embargo, the ownership of natural resources was of declining importance.[2] The growing free market for raw materials, substitution, and recycling made domestic sources of raw materials less crucial. Japan was living proof of the ability of a nation to industrialize and grow economically without indigenous resources. Until just recently, when OPEC forced a sizable rise in the price of oil, the Japanese example seemed to show that possession of natural resources was all but unnecessary. Thus, a variable that has been of steadily declining importance has assumed, once again, a more important place in the power equation as a result of recent events. At this juncture, its future role is uncertain.

At present there is no evidence that resource substitution will not continue as it has in the past. Technology now makes more substitution possible than ever before. Clearly, iron and coal are less important than they were in the past. Recently, oil has become a crucial resource, but due to the pollution problem and the development of solar and fusion energy, it probably will not remain such an important source of energy in most countries. In general, the free market situation for buying and selling of almost all resources—with the exception of petroleum—has changed very little. A number of nations have tried to form resource cartels, but with the exception of OPEC, their efforts have been unsuccessful. There is little reason to predict that new attempts will be fruitful. Obtaining resources from the sea and recycling offer tremendous possibilities for reducing the importance of assured sources of raw materials in the future.

In this context, several new factors seem relevant when discussing the advantage of a natural resource base to world-power status. First, the natural resource reserves must be large, making possible sufficient quantities for domestic use plus exports in order for them to be a source of international influence. To a nation without exceptional riches, with low population-to-resource base and/or little or no industrialization, a large reserve base offers advantages to world-power status by guaranteeing some self-reliance, but it is not a magic source of investment capital. Second, having advanced technology which would permit the acquisition of resources from the sea or the devising of substitutes for scarce or expensive resources is a vital asset. Third, the ability to influence world transport and trade, store up resources, and thus affect prices and in other ways control or influence markets is a source of world power. Self-sufficiency per se is not very crucial since industrialization and self-sufficiency are now antithetical.

Clearly, China is rich in natural resources when compared to most of the other second-ranking powers. However, China does not have a good resource base in per capita terms. For China to sell resources while its industrial development proceeds at a rapid pace will be impossible. Australia, Canada, and the oil-producing countries of the Middle East will improve their world-power status markedly, based upon the resource asset. Most of the underpopulated, underdeveloped countries will also make gains. However, it cannot be expected that China will enhance its world role by resource sales. China has sufficient resources for its own development and is more self-sufficient than other second-ranking nations. But, as was noted above, these factors are now of less importance, and will probably remain so in the future. And China has very limited capabilities to acquire resources from the sea, to substitute, or to control the market on any resource.

China's efforts to industrialize and its economic growth in general, although impressive when juxtaposed with its past, must be considered meager in the context of China's drive to become a world power. In the first five or six years after 1949, the regime engineered impressive progress in both areas. But China's industrialization process soon ran into snags. Since the late 1950s Chinese leaders have deemphasized industrialization and have given greater stress to agricultural development, which, although probably a wise decision, certainly limits China's prospects of becoming a world economic power. At the present time China cannot be regarded as a modern industrial power, and there is little reason to think that it will become one in the near future. One major impediment to China's future economic growth is that many nations have developed labor-intensive industries—currently China's main hope for industrialization—making the competition in this area severe.[3] Thus, while China is now making renewed efforts to become an industrial nation, it is obvious that China is in the race late, and the advantage to be gained in terms of global influence is not as marked as it was two decades ago.

China's economic development, in general terms, is likewise not impressive if it is judged as a means whereby Peking can enhance its global status. Even though China has seemingly resolved the problems of poverty, disease, and hunger, it is still a poor country. When its economic growth, using increases in gross national product as a benchmark, is compared to that of Japan or West Germany, China's record is poor. It does not even look impressive when compared to India. For the last two decades, China's economic growth rate has been close to or less than the world's average. Certain built-in barriers—such as a low land-to-population ratio, insufficient capital, and ideological impediments—seem to determine that this will remain true in the near, and probably the distant, future.

Worse may be said of China's performance in the sphere of science and technology. The gap between China and most other second-ranking powers is tremendous. And China is making little progress, if any at all, in closing the gap. China's educational system is not producing enough trained scientists, while its budget for research and other scientific work, in relative or comparative terms, is low. Ideology presents a serious obstacle to progress in science and technology. China has built atomic bombs and missiles, but these accomplishments stem from borrowed technology and singularly devoted efforts. Unlike such countries as France, Japan, and the United States and, to a lesser extent, the United Kingdom and West Germany, China's technological development is not encouraged by close ties to consumer industries; nor is there a spread effect from government-sponsored projects. These factors, plus the fact that technology is now a less freely acquired asset, means that China's future progress in this realm is far from promising.

In the past, industrialization and economic growth were considered major variables in the makeup of great powers; the development of science and technology in and of itself was not. More recently, however, industrialization has become clearly less important. A number of countries have built strong economies without an industrial base. This probably will occur even more in the future. Economic growth in general, however, remains an important factor since trade, aid, and investment remain important avenues of influence in international politics. The same may be said of science and technology—but to an even greater degree. Of all the ingredients of power, the science and technology factor has grown in magnitude and importance in recent years more than any other, and this trend undoubtedly will continue, probably into the distant future.[4] Thus, over the short run at least, and probably over the long run, China has a serious handicap to overcome in making gains in world-power status.

In the realm of military power, China outranks the other medium-level powers in some respects and even compares favorably to the superpowers. In military manpower China rates with the superpowers and far outranks the other second-ranking powers. Also, it has nuclear weapons and missile delivery systems that only two other second-level powers— France and the United Kingdom—possess. However, the contribution of China's large army to its overall military strength is severely reduced by lack of logistical capabilities. Similarly, China's nuclear forces do not present a credible threat to most other second-level powers or to the United States, due to China's lack of ICBMs. Meanwhile, an international agreement, namely the 1968 Nuclear Nonproliferation Treaty, protects the nonnuclear countries from China's nuclear threat. Taking cognizance of these realities and the fact that nuclear weapons have not been used since World War II, and then by only one country, they are doubtless less important in assessing China's military power than is usually thought. On the conventional war level, China's inability to use its forces distant from its borders because of the lack of transport facilities is a major limitation to its global military influence. So is its inflexibility in terms of weapons and tactics. Most of the other second-ranking powers have greater capabilities in this realm than China, particularly France and the United Kingdom. Perhaps most important, in terms of future global influence based upon military power, is the ability to fight wars by proxy: China's capabilities are limited here by its inability to give sophisticated or large amounts of military aid, and this will likely remain so in the future.

China's nuclear power status will no doubt continue to afford Peking some global influence and may increase perceptibly when China attains an ICBM, although it has been argued that when China builds an intercontinental missile it will evoke a reaction in the United States either to build a compensating antimissile system or to stop new military technology from going to China, and it is for this reason that the Chinese have not already built an ICBM and perhaps will not in the near future.[5] Its large army makes China an Asian power, but in firepower terms, China is far outranked by the two superpowers, even in East and Southeast Asia, and it is unlikely that this will change in the foreseeable future—if ever.[6] Finally, China's military influence in Asia, which at one time was formidable, is now offset by the military presence of India and Japan as well as the Soviet Union and the United States. Thus, China's so-called outstanding assets in the realm of military strength must be qualified.

It should be noted also that military influence overall is a decreasingly important factor in measuring national power capabilities.[7] Strategic power has not been employed for over three decades in any real sense, and in few cases has superior conventional power played a crucial role in world politics. If strategic power remains a significant part of the global power balance, which it probably will in more subtle ways, the superpowers will continue to maintain supreme prerogatives that second-ranking powers, especially China, cannot challenge. Only the United States and the Soviet Union can afford to continue the arms race, and only those two powers have the necessary broad scientific and technological base, as well as the various other resources needed to compete in a global arms race, to be classified as superpowers. Meanwhile, other facets or components of military power are increasing in importance: military aid, intervention capabilities, and intelligence gathering. These capabilities require a high level of technology and money to maintain and, again, the gap between the two superpowers and other second-ranking powers seems to be permanent. In any case, China is not an outstanding competitor, even among the second-level powers, in these areas, and a sanguine view of its future potential certainly is not warranted.

In the realm of political stability, diplomacy, and will, China's strengths and weaknesses are subject to even greater speculation. Many writers have accredited China with considerable strength based upon its centralized, totalitarian political system. Mao indeed built a movement that united China as it never had been before. Many of the problems that kept China a weak nation in the past were overcome by the new regime, and the Chinese people were thoroughly indoctrinated to follow the commands of the new leadership. The image of China as a sleeping dragon that, when awakened, would cause the world serious problems made this appear awesome. Of course, due to the fact that China is a closed nation, there is little counterevidence available to refute the argument that China is now unified and the rulers' control over the Chinese masses complete. Nevertheless, in contrast to the 1950s, the second and third decades of Communist rule in China have presented a different image.

China's diplomacy has a similar history. After initial successes based upon its alliance with Moscow, followed by diplomatic initiatives toward the Afro-Asian world at Bandung in 1955, China's diplomacy went through a series of ups and downs. In subsequent years its feud with Moscow undermined China's relations with most of the Communist bloc. Similarly, Peking's aggression against India alienated much of the Third World. Then, activities during the Cultural Revolution made Peking appear to be irrational and out of touch with global realities. After the Cultural Revolution, China returned to "normalcy"; but it remains questionable how much success China will have as a contender for leadership of the Third World, in playing one superpower off against the other, or increasing its influence in the United Nations and other international organizations. Most analysts feel that China should be recognized as a legitimate world power; but few consider China a major diplomatic force in world politics.

Concerning the ambitions and will of China's leaders, a positive image was also built up in the 1950s. A stable domestic scene and effective economic planning, in contrast to the situation in China before 1949, made it appear that China's new leaders were single-minded and determined. In addition, Mao continued to build a strong military organization even after he consolidated his control of China's mainland and made aggressive statements toward the outside world. And he seemed to have explicit plans upon which to base actions. Yet neither Mao's statements nor his goals have turned out to be very meaningful. China has not regarded atomic bombs as paper tigers. Peking has made no serious efforts to regain lost territories. In the face of threats by the Kremlin, China sought detente with the United States. And in recent years Chinese leaders have given little real support to wars of national liberation.

So although the political ingredient of national power is increasing in importance, it is not clear that China has made gains over its competitors. Its record in the 1950s was good; in the 1960s it was not. At present China's political system and its ideology still cause China to be regarded as a pariah or renegade by many countries, offsetting the advantages gained from maintaining internal control. Likewise, its pride and xenophobia enhance Chinese nationalism and promote self-respect; but at the same time it causes other countries to fear China. And, while China's global political influence may be expected to increase in the future by virtue of the fact that it has long been excluded from participation in the United Nations and most other world organizations, nothing spectacular should be expected. For several reasons it cannot be anticipated that Peking will gain leadership over the poor countries of the world: lack of unity among these nations and their reliance upon the developed nations; competition from India, and other important Third World nations; and China's lack of capabilities in aid and trade and need to tie its own economic development to that of the developed nations. China will also continue to find its views on international law and diplomacy unorthodox, and this will serve as a barrier to greater participation in world affairs. Similarly, it seems inevitable that China will become a more open nation in the future, and as this happens, outside influences can be expected to cause some disruption to internal cohesion and control.

In summary, then, if we assess China's status as a world power in terms of the elements of power as they apply to the contemporary world, China's strengths lie primarily in areas that are less relevant to world-power status than in the past. In the ingredients of power that will be more important in the future, China is weakest. However, it is also necessary to analyze China's power capabilities in the context of current international political relations, noting the special areas or categories of international influence. By so doing, it will be clearer how important the defects in China's power capabilities are and easier to determine its potential or future rank in the hierarchy of nations.

If we look at power differently—that is, from the perspective of a nation's capacity to participate directly in the global political arena and influence the rules or structure of international politics—another style of analysis is possible. Here the ingredients of power are seen almost exclusively from the perspective of their use. When a nation acts in the international system, there are four kinds of influence that it can exert: strategic military, conventional military (both military categories include population and geography as well as some of the other factors just discussed), economic (which includes resources and technology), and political.[8] Clearly, the superpowers possess all four types of influences or capabilities; the small powers do not possess any of them. The middle-range powers have capabilities that vary in amounts and types.

Strategic power may be defined generally as weapons of mass destruction that can be used to destroy other nations or cripple them permanently and thus affect the makeup of the system. By virtue of possessing such weapons, certain actors play a special role in international politics. To have significant strategic power requires the ability to destroy any other power, even if attacked first—a second-strike capability. Clearly, only the United States and the Soviet Union possess such power. There are four other nuclear powers, but none of them are close to making a breakthrough in attaining an assured unacceptable destruction capability vis-à-vis either or both of the superpowers. India is the farthest away, since it has yet to build nuclear bombs even though it has tested a nuclear device. The United Kingdom is not really in the race because of its close defense ties with the United States. China and France are the closest to becoming strategic powers, and France, because of its better delivery systems—missiles with solid fuel propellants, nuclear submarines, and multiple, independently targeted warheads—is probably the closer of the two. However, considerable evidence suggests that both have opted out of the contest to become genuine strategic powers. For at least ten years, neither has been able to devote the funds necessary to keep up with the superpowers in the arms race. Neither has made progress in building the next generation of weapons, such as orbital bombs and lasers. France, by its own admission that it cannot afford to continue to compete, and the fact that it has not projected sufficient funds for research and development to do so, seems to be dropping out. Peking's situation is similar; it has also failed to devote the resources and funding for a new generation of weapons. And when it says it is not a superpower and will not become one, it seems to be saying the same thing as France—that it is dropping out of the race.

Thus, when assessing the nature of strategic power, it appears that the superpowers will retain their advantage in this realm, and that in strategic terms the international system is not evolving away from bipolarity. Washington and Moscow have a monopoly of strategic force authority, and it seems unlikely that this will change. No other power, including China—which is not even the closest—will be able to alter this situation.

China, like three other second-ranking powers, is able to garner some prestige by virtue of possessing atomic weapons. But it has become obvious that a large number of other countries, including many that we regard as third- or fourth-ranking powers, can become nuclear powers easily. Thus nuclear status is now seen to change very little the makeup of the global power balance.

In the realm of conventional military power, China must be considered a major actor of sorts. Problems of logistics and lack of a navy by which it could use its conventional power distant from its borders, however, make China a relevant conventional military power only in Asia, and in limited areas there. Put simply, China's military power is a major factor only in areas that are physically contiguous with China. However, for special reasons, China has less influence in border areas than the size and reputation of its military would suggest. Its military power is of little value on its northern border because it is more than matched by Soviet power. Mountains, India's military power, and New Delhi's alliance with the Soviet Union limit China's impact on its southwest border. For a long time the United States countered China's military influence beyond its borders to the southeast. Now a combination of U.S. and Soviet strategic and conventional military power—plus India, Japan, Vietnam, and the Association of Southeast Asian Nations (a regional organization with mutual defense interests)—offsets what might otherwise be a sphere of influence in terms of conventional military power for China.

In terms of economic influence, China is far from being a major contender. China is outranked in terms of economic power by more than five nations and a number of economic and regional organizations. If trade, control of international commerce, and influence in global finance or money markets are figured in the economic power equation, or if economic influence is defined so as to include these other variables, which most analysts agree is the case, China ranks below ten to fifteen other actors. And it is questionable that China will improve its position. The nations with which China must compete are growing economically as fast as China; the superpowers are so far ahead that the gap will not be closed in the foreseeable future. Meanwhile, the world is experiencing the rise of new economic actors. Western Europe is already exerting economic power almost equal to that of the superpowers. OPEC has displayed what some regard as superpower economic influence. The multinational corporations are also a major world economic actor. Others are coming. Thus, China in the future will compete not only with national economic powers but also with regional actors, cartels and international corporations. All of these are acquiring global economic influence faster than China.

In the realm of political power, China has demonstrated few special talents when compared to other actors or in the context of today's changing world. If political power is taken to mean something beyond simply a combination of the other forms of power—and to refer to such things as innovation or leadership in political development, diplomacy, culture, academics, religion, and communications—China has little claim to fame. In the realm of political development, the Western democracies and, to a lesser extent, the Soviet Union have the most to offer. The same is true of diplomacy. In culture, the West, especially the United States, is a world leader. Intellectually, the West is again the prime mover in the world, together with the Soviet Union and Japan. As world religious leaders, the United States, Israel, India, and several of the Middle Eastern countries have disproportionate influence. In communications and control of the media again the West dominates, especially the United States and the United Kingdom. Australia, Canada, France, Japan, West Germany, and even Hong Kong provide more input into the global mass media than China. In none of the realms just mentioned does China have special influence or a potential to gain influence. Yet all of them are important components of political power.

In addition to seeking conclusions concerning China's world-power role in terms of trends in the importance of various elements of power, or reducing the ingredients of national power to more specific categories of international influence, we should also look at the structure and workings of the international system, which serves as the environment or arena in which nations interact and endeavor to exercise their influence. The nature and rules of the system aid some nations and inhibit others. The system also affects which kinds of power are most useful. Finally, changes in the international system determine new rules and future means of influence as well as dictate what nations or actors will play larger or smaller roles. Over the last decade or more the system has grown away from tight bipolarity toward loose bipolarity. Multipolarity and universality are currently evolving characteristics of the global system. At present the system probably can be described as a mixture of loose bipolar, multipolar, and universal traits, with less emphasis on the latter. The bipolar nature of the system, though perhaps resistant to change in the strategic military sense, probably will continue to evolve toward a multipolar structure. What impacts or effects will this transformation have?

The evolution of multipolarity can be expected to produce four major influences on international politics: conflict will increase in frequency but decrease in intensity; the level of interaction among nations will increase; the arms race will dampen; and the importance of ideology will diminish.[9] An examination of each of these changes is telling in terms of the future importance of the various elements or categories of national strength.

Increasing numbers of limited wars or conflagrations will tend to give an advantage to those nations with effective intelligence systems; a flexibility of military capability, especially a navy and logistics capabilities; the capacity to purvey a broad spectrum of weapons, especially new and highly technical weapons; control of the media to influence world opinion; and diplomatic talents.[10] Clearly, the advantage goes to the superpowers, Western nations, technologically and scientifically advanced nations, English-speaking nations, and nations with allies.

Almost the same may be said of the increasing interaction among nations, though military capabilities will not be so important and trade will increase in relevance. Nations that export culture will also exert a greater influence, and open nations will be advantaged as opposed to those that are closed.[11] The Western nations and Japan will benefit from this trend the most in terms of an improvement in their power status. Leaders of blocs, members of important blocs, and intellectual and cultural leaders will gain. The Soviet Union will lose. The United States will lose some of its authority as a superpower, but will gain in other respects. China will gain by virtue of the fact that alliance systems may decline in importance and because its isolation has limited China's global influence; in other ways, China will probably lose. In this case, a balance sheet reflecting China's overall gain or loss is difficult to draw. Certainly a high degree of optimism is not warranted.

A slowing of the arms race would influence negatively the importance of strategic weapons and the role of the superpowers and major second-ranking powers, especially the nuclear ones. A disincentive would also be generated against other powers obtaining strategic weapons.[12] This trend will reduce the importance of the United States and the Soviet Union in world politics, but it will reduce the importance of the other nuclear powers even more. On the other hand, it may give the superpowers a permanent strategic advantage and thus ultimate control over the system. In other words, the system may continue to become multipolar, making weapons of mass destruction less a measure of power, but this will affect the second-ranking powers first and more intensely. This trend will be to the distinct disadvantage of powers that have or are building strategic weapons but are not, or cannot become, superpowers. China, along with France, will be a major loser.

Finally, there will be a decline of ideology as the global system becomes multipolar and particularly as it becomes universal.[13] This will operate to weaken the roles of the superpowers and other "ideological" states. The United States has already grappled with this problem and, to a considerable extent, has adjusted. It probably will continue to have some weakening influence upon the United States, but much more upon the Soviet Union. In the case of both superpowers, however, this can be compensated for by increasing cultural, diplomatic, and other instrumentalities of influence. Other ideological nations and regional leaders will be disadvantaged. Nonideological powers able to wield other forms of influence will gain. China will be a major loser.

If multipolarity is only a temporary or transitional phase and the system eventually evolves into a universal one (and there is considerable evidence to suggest that meaningful progress is being made in that direction if functionalism rather than global centralized political control is the criterion of judgment), the result will be a decline in the importance of strategic, conventional military, and economic power. Commensurately, political power will increase in importance. In other words, the nations with diplomatic, cultural, intellectual, and communications capabilities will enhance their world roles. The influence of a number of international organizations as well as numerous nonpolitical international actors will also increase. Thus, nations that play important roles in global organizations will benefit. It is also likely that the transition toward a universal system will encourage the development of regional organizations and, for a time, enhance the roles of regional leaders.[14] None of these trends clearly favors China.

The evolution of the system toward a multipolar structure or even toward universalism is not an auspicious trend where Peking's desire to play a greater role in world politics is concerned. On the other hand, due to the fact that China is responsible for the weakening of bipolarity, its influence during the transition phase, which may be the next ten years, may be a special one. It may be expected that China's role in the United Nations, and perhaps its voice in international politics in general, will improve somewhat for the next few years because of the ending of its isolationist foreign policy and the changed policy of the United States toward Peking. But this can be only temporary. Likewise, China may experience somewhat faster economic growth for the next few years if Maoist impediments to growth are eradicated and it can improve its trade ties with the West. External finance and borrowing or buying technology will also help, but this depends upon good relations with the West. Détente between Washington and Moscow limits China's possibilities. In any case, it cannot be expected that the United States will help China become a superpower. Rather it may be that the U.S. is willing to help China because it views this as unlikely.

The conclusions made above are in marked contrast to most views held about China's future role as a world power. However, they are in consonance with the empirical evidence available concerning China's power capabilities, and take into consideration trends in the importance of the various factors of power and the context in which they will have to operate, namely, a multipolar situation. The overestimation of China's power, particularly its potential power and its ability to assume an important place in world politics, arises from a variety of misconceptions, some unwarranted assumptions, and a generally superficial view of what constitutes power and influence in international relations. Some of these need to be mentioned in view of the fact that most analysts estimate China's role to be greater.

One problem with using the traditional elements of power as a measuring stick to assess China's capabilities is that they were designed primarily to compare nations' power rather than to measure it quantitatively; consequently, they apply better to measuring the relative strengths of nations that are similar in size and level of development.[15] In short, the formula was designed to weigh the relative warmaking potentials of several European nations and has not been adequately revised. China is different in so many ways that such comparisons, to a large extent lose their validity. Also, the elements-of-power concept was originally employed to predict which nations would win in a conventional war, while assuming that all nations were planning for this eventuality. Thus, the sole purpose of power was seen to be victory in war. The power concept also was used to ascertain the strength of allies and the need for nations to break or change alliances in a balance-of-power situation. All of the nations involved possessed weapons of near similar sophistication, used similar military tactics, and abided by certain rules of war. Now war involves more than the use of conventional armies, and it includes much more than actual combat. At the present time it is questionable to what extent nations, consciously or otherwise, prepare for war. In short, there is little resemblance between the past balance-of-power system and the present bipolar system. The future world system will be even more different.

These misunderstandings of the elements-of-power formula have led to an absolute view or to an overemphasis on some of the elements of power and the devaluation or exclusion of others. For example, it was generally assumed that any increase in population or territory would have an equally positive influence upon power status. As a result, the importance of population and territory was overstated. The same is true of the components of economic and military power: the level of industrialization and the manpower of the standing army were given too much weight. Similarly, iron and coal were seen as natural resources of overriding importance because they were essential factors to building heavy industry, which laid the foundation for economic growth. Economic growth, it was also argued, brought profits that could buy or build armies. These misconceptions make China appear to have greater power capabilities than would be the case otherwise.

Another assumption frequently made when assessing power capabilities is that the international system has no relevance or is static. As we have already noted, the concept of the elements of power was designed for the balance-of-power system. It does not work so neatly in a bipolar system. And when it is applied there, it gives the appearance that all second-ranking powers seek superpower status and the closer they are to attaining it the greater will be their efforts. It also assumes that at some point in time they will make it, as long as they are catching up with the superpowers in strategic weapons, or gaining on the superpowers in most or all other power components over the long run. This neglects the transitional nature of the international system in the direction of multipolarity and universality, or assumes that the same situation applies there. Thus, China's strategic weapons are given excessive importance, as is its ability to join the ranks of the superpowers.

It should be noted in this connection that there is a contradiction involved between attaining superpower status and the evolution toward a multipolar system. Weakening the superpowers means that the rules of the system will change, making it more difficult for a growing power to gain superpower prerogatives or status. China had considerable influence in forcing the system to move from bipolarity to multipolarity, even though coincidently. But even though China's efforts were successful, the effect was to create a system which reduced the importance of super-powers as well as the ability of aspiring nations to gain superpower status or prerogatives. Moreover, most observers failed to see that the results were not in China's favor.

Another error that has resulted in overappraising China's power status is the assumption that rules are nonexistent in the international system or that the system is characterized by chaos. Thus it is thought that any nation having the will to play a role in international politics, assuming it has moderate capabilities, will succeed. Hence, China's historical role, together with Mao's ambitious-sounding statements, give the false im-pression that China is a major force in international politics, in potential if not in real terms. In reality, the influence of the system's rules and world culture upon nations' behavior is greater than general observa-tions suggest. This explains in part why China has found it difficult to play a role in international politics, and why its ambitions and threats have not been very relevant to its global influence.

Finally, China's role has been exaggerated because of its own claims to greatness, as reflected in the publication of production figures and eco-nomic growth rates and the persistent covering-up of poor performance or setbacks. China's fairly impressive accomplishments through the first five years of the new regime also made a lasting impression, to some extent advertised by China's adversaries. The latter accepted both Pe-king's accomplishments and its threats at face value and sometimes exag-gerated them. Some assistance also was provided by admirers on the left of the political spectrum, who saw Chinese ideology as new and fresh and an alternative to American capitalism and Soviet communism. They hoped that China would become a great power, and they transformed their hopes to expectations.

Once all of this is understood, it is clear that China is not destined to be a superpower, a one-half superpower, or even a top-ranking or special-ranking second-level power. What, then, is its status or position among the hierarchy of powers? And what role will China play in international politics in the future?

China should be regarded as one of a number of second-ranking na-tional powers—such as France, Japan, the United Kingdom, West Ger-many, and perhaps Australia, Brazil, Canada, India, and Italy. In terms of its national power alone, China ranks generally among the first group and above the second group. Its formal role in world affairs has been low compared to the first group because of its isolationism, although in the early 1970s this changed rather quickly. As a nation-state China will probably play a formal role in world politics similar to its present role and close to that of the other high-ranking second-level powers.

Since international politics has become increasingly complex, it is perhaps also useful to speak of ways in which China will play an important role in international affairs and, conversely, ways in which China will play a lesser or insignificant role. This will perhaps make possible a more accurate assessment of China's current and future role in international politics.

China will not attain superpower status. However, because of its special role in fostering the decline of the bipolar system, it may maintain the role it already has assumed to some extent as the conscience of the superpowers. In other words China may ensure that they do not regress to earlier modes of behavior or attitudes that characterized their roles in the bipolar system. China may even assume a leadership role among non-superpower nations in this respect, and guarantee, to some extent, that the international system will continue to evolve into multipolarity. This role, however, should not be overrated, since the development of multipolarity was based primarily upon trends that were influenced very little by China's efforts to change the system and which in any case can be regarded as inevitable. The future evolution of the system will probably transpire in a similar way.

By virtue of its nuclear status, China may play some role in limiting the testing and use of nuclear weapons and disarmament. So far, China has been excluded from arms limitation and disarmament talks. Peking should be included, and doubtless will be, in decision making in this realm in the future.

China may also be regarded as one among several leaders of the Third World nations. Such a leadership position is not as important as some would assume, however; the Third World is not united and probably will not be in the future. Therefore, the so-called Third World bloc probably will not be an important force in international affairs for some time to come, if ever. Also, China will compete with several other nations for leadership prerogatives and, in most cases, probably will not assume a dominant position. Peking may likewise try to represent the poor nations of the world against the rich. But similar problems arise here. On some issues, such as aid and controlling world markets, China may be able to speak for the underdeveloped nations, but this will probably be chiefly on an issue-by-issue basis.

China may serve as a model for economic development that does not foster wide gaps between rich and poor or consider social inequality an acceptable condition. Similarly, China may stand as an example of population control—if its birth control programs succeed and its leadership decides that such a role is worthwhile. But in these cases, or any others, it is questionable how much other countries will emulate China, and even if they do, how much influence will accrue to Peking.

China is and will remain one of three or more Asian regional powers. Thus, it has a voice in Asian affairs and will continue to influence the course of events within the region. However, it will not become the dominant power in Asia, and probably will enhance its influence in the long term only by cooperation with other Asian powers and the superpowers, or at least one of them. In the short term it will continue to possess considerable disruptive potential in the area, but this cannot be translated into much benefit for China or into lasting influence.

China's role in international economic affairs is negligible and probably will remain so. This is also true of its role in science and technology and in communications and culture. It has, and will continue to maintain, a bit more influence in global legal and political affairs, but its role here cannot be expected to expand appreciably in the future. Its role in the United Nations probably will grow somewhat over the short run but decline thereafter. Its leadership of a special brand of communism and some revolutionary movements is worth mentioning, but is deteriorating and no doubt will continue to decline in the future.

In short, we should expect China to play the role of a major power at times and exert very little influence at other times. The variations will be considerable. China is, and will continue to be, a unique country with important contributions to make in the realms of global stability and peace. However, we should not expect China to act consistently as a major power—even most of the time—or play a role generally beyond that of the second-ranking powers. We certainly should not anticipate, hope, or fear that China will seriously alter the course or nature of world politics in the future.

Notes

CHAPTER 1

1. This view is also reflected in the opinions and comments of leaders such as Napoleon, Lenin, and Franklin Roosevelt. Their opinions, however, generally reflect the historical view of cyclic patterns of history in East and West.

2. A number of writers have argued that the Chinese Communists were the first to effectively capture the spirit of Chinese nationalism and have continued to utilize this potent force. See, for example, A. Doak Barnett, *Communist China and Asia: Challenge to American Foreign Policy* (New York: Harper & Brothers, 1960), p. 67.

3. For a presentation of the totalitarian model and its application to China, see Carl Friedrich and Zbigniew Brzezinski, *Totalitarian Dictatorship and Autocracy* (New York: Praeger, 1961), chapter 8.

4. See Peter Van Ness, *Revolution and Chinese Foreign Policy: Peking's Support for Wars of National Liberation* (Berkeley: University of California Press, 1970), chapter 3. This point, as well as a discussion of Chinese nationalism and the totalitarian system, will be discussed further in chapter 6.

5. See Choh-ming Li, *Economic Development of Communist China* (Berkeley: University of California Press, 1959) for a description of China's economy during the first several years of the Mao regime that is quite optimistic.

6. An exaggerated view of China's influence in weakening the international influence of the Soviet Union and the United States is presented in a book written by members of the Committee of Concerned Asian Scholars after a short visit to China in 1972. See *China: Inside the People's Republic* (New York: Bantam Books, 1972).

7. *Ibid.*

8. Various writers have speculated on the effect of China's joining the international community in terms of a new or altered international system. For a discussion of tripolarity as the outcome, see Ronald J. Yalem, "Tripolarity and the International System," *Orbis*, Winter 1972. A much broader discussion is found in Harold C. Hinton, *Three and A Half Powers: The New Balance of Powers in Asia* (Bloomington: Indiana University Press, 1975).

9. Various views that China is not a major world power and is unlikely to become one are presented in following chapters. Therefore, no specific views are noted here.

10. A. F. K. Organski, *World Politics* (New York: Alfred A. Knopf, 1968).

11. Karl W. Deutsch, "On the Concepts of Politics and Power," *Journal of International Affairs*, no. 2 (1967).

12. Steven L. Spiegel, *Dominance and Diversity: The International Hierarchy* (Boston: Little, Brown, 1960), pp. 239–40.

13. See Wayne H. Ferris, *The Power Capabilities of Nation-States* (Lexington, Mass.: D. C. Heath, 1973), p. 37, for a view of power status that weighs heavily the science and technology factor.

14. Katherine Organski and A. F. K. Organski, *Population and World Power* (New York: Alfred A. Knopf, 1969), pp. 239–40.

15. In addition to the authors already mentioned that discuss elements or components of national power, see Robert A. Dahl, "The Concept of Power," *Behavioral Sciences*, July 1957; F. C. German, "A Tentative Evaluation of World Power," *Journal of Conflict Revolution*, March 1960; F. H. Hinsley, *Power and the Pursuit of Peace* (Cambridge: Cambridge University Press, 1963); K. J. Holsti, *International Politics* (Englewood Cliffs, N.J.: Prentice-Hall, 1967); Klaus Knorr, *The War Potential of Nations* (New York: Basic Books, 1975); Hans J. Morgenthau, *Politics Among Nations: The Struggle for Power and Peace* (New York: Alfred A. Knopf, 1974); Harold and Margaret Sprout, *Foundations of International Politics* (New York: D. Van Nostrand, 1962); and N. J. Spykman, *America's Strategy in World Politics* (New Haven: Yale University Press, 1942).

16. For further details on this point, as well as a discussion that gives importance to geography and population, see Morgenthau, *Politics Among Nations*, pp. 112–14, 124–28.

17. Some writers argue that China is in a favored geopolitical location because it is in the center of the largest continent. Others, however, note that China is not blessed by geography since it has more nations on its borders and more unnatural boundaries than any other country. Also, it has the longest border with another country and that country, the Soviet Union, is an enemy. This point will be discussed in greater detail in the next chapter.

18. Both Morgenthau, *Politics Among Nations*, and Deutsch, "On the Concepts of Politics and Power," emphasize the importance of this element of power.

19. For an assessment of power that stresses the economic factor, see Bruce Russett, *Trends in World Politics* (New York: Macmillan, 1969).

20. Emphasis on the military factor can be found in Inis Claude, Jr., *Power and International Relations* (New York: Random House, 1962). Also, see Morgenthau, *Politics Among Nations*.

21. Knorr, *The War Potential of Nations*, stresses the importance of political stability, although he argues that no specific type of system is generally advantageous over any other. Morgenthau, *Politics Among Nations*, gives considerable weight to a nation's diplomacy. D. O. Wilkinson, *Comparative Foreign Relations: Framework and Methods* (Belmont, Calif.: Dickenson Press, 1969), and Raymond Aron, *Peace and War: A Thesis of International Relations* (New York: Doubleday, 1966), note the importance of the will of the people.

22. See Ferris, *The Power Capabilities of Nation-States*, and Victor Basiuk, "The Impact of Technology in the Next Decades," *Orbis*, Spring 1970.

CHAPTER 2

1. For a further discussion on the problems of land use in China, see Theodore Shabed, *China's Changing Map* (New York: Praeger Publishers, 1956), chapter 1.

2. About 3 percent of the land in China not under cultivation can be reclaimed. See *National Basic Intelligence Factbook* (Washington, D.C.: Central Intelligence Agency, January 1977). Also, see Jan S. Prybyla, "The Asian Dilemma: Reordering National Priorities," *Current History*, June 1975, for an analysis of the implications of this problem.

3. See Owen L. Dawson, *Communist China's Agriculture: Its Development and Future Potential* (New York: Praeger Publishers, 1970), chapter 4, and Michael Freeberne, "Physical and Social Geography," in *The Far East and Australia, 1977—78* (London: Europa, 1977), p. 287.

4. John Bryan Starr, *Ideology and Culture: An Introduction to the Dialectic of Contemporary Chinese Politics* (New York: Harper & Row, 1973), p. 56.

5. Charles Robert Roll, Jr., and Kung-chia Yeh, "Balance in Coastal and Inland Industrial Development," in *China: A Reassessment of the Economy* (Washington, D.C.: Joint Economic Committee of the U.S. Congress, 1975).

6. This point is discussed in a number of texts on international relations. For a recent discussion in the Asian context, see Robert A. Scalapino, *Asia and the Road Ahead: Issues for the Major Powers* (Berkeley: University of California Press, 1975), p. 254.

7. Spiegel, *Dominance and Diversity*, p. 43.

8. See Harold C. Hinton, *Communist China in World Politics* (Boston: Houghton Mifflin, 1966), chapters 11 and 12, for a discussion of China's borders with the various nations of South and Southeast Asia.

9. See Dick Wilson, *Anatomy of China* (New York: Mentor Books, 1967), chapter 8.

10. "People's Republic of China: Handbook of Economic Indicators," *Central Intelligence Agency Research Aid*, (Washington, D.C.: August 1976).

11. Alexander Eckstein, *China's Economic Revolution* (Cambridge: Cambridge University Press, 1977), p. 228.

12. Barry M. Richman, *Industrial Society in Communist China* (New York: Random House, 1969), p. 376.

13. Ashley J. Coale and Edgar M. Hoover, *Population Growth and Economic Development in Low Income Countries* (Princeton: Princeton University Press, 1958), p. 30.

14. See *United Nations Statistical Yearbook, 1975* for population growth in all countries.

15. *Encyclopedia Americana Yearbook, 1976*, p. 457. The *United Nations Statistical Yearbook, 1977* cites China's population growth as 1.7 per thousand per year and India's as 2.1. This would make it possible for India to surpass China in population size in about 40 years.

16. See Judith Banister, "International Effects of China's Population Situation,"

in Bryant G. Garth, ed., *China's Changing Role in the World Economy* (New York: Praeger Publishers, 1975), pp. 98–101. The author even ties China's overpopulation problem to the killing of overseas Chinese in some Southeast Asian countries.

17. For an account of the Chinese government's changing stance on birth control and its inconsistencies in reporting such data, see Leo A. Orleans, "China's Population Statistics: An Illusion?" *China Quarterly*, January-March 1965.

18. The world's coastline is 312,000 kilometers. China's coastline of about 4,200 is only a little more than 1 percent of the total—compared to its population, which is over 21 percent. Its territorial sea, using the 200-mile claim as a basis, is considerably smaller than that of the Soviet Union, the United States, Australia, Canada, and a dozen other countries. For further information on this point, see "Theoretical Area Allocations of Seabed to Coastal States" (Washington, D.C.: U.S. Department of State, August 12, 1972).

CHAPTER 3

1. *United Nations Statistical Yearbook, 1975*, p. 95.

2. Alva Lewis Erisman, "China: Agriculture in the 1970s," in *China: A Reassessment of the Economy* (Washington, D.C.: U.S. Congress Joint Economic Committee, July 1975), p. 348.

3. For a synopsis of China's recent agricultural performance, see Kuan-i Chen, "Agricultural Modernization and Modernization in China," *Current History*, September 1976.

4. Jan Deleyne, *The Chinese Economy* (New York: Harper & Row, 1971), p. 63.

5. Dwight H. Perkins, "Constraints Influencing China's Agricultural Performance," in *China: A Reassessment of the Economy*, p. 353.

6. Ibid.

7. Banister, "International Effects of Chinese Population Situation," in Garth, ed., *China's Changing Role in the World Economy*, p. 94.

8. Perkins, "Constraints Influencing China's Agricultural Performance," in *China: A Reassessment of the Economy*, p. 350. It is also worth noting that 20 to 25 percent of the grain harvested in underdeveloped countries is lost to birds, insects, and rotting. China, on the other hand, has virtually overcome these problems.

9. Colin Clark, *Starvation or Plenty?* (New York: Taplinger, 1972), p. 66.

10. *Peking Review*, December 15, 1972.

11. According to one estimate, there are 7,000,000 square kilometers (1.7 billion acres) in underdeveloped countries that can be cultivated. In addition, irrigation in these countries is less than 50 percent efficient. See D. Gale Johnson, *World Food Problems and Prospects* (Washington, D.C.: American Enterprise Institute, 1975), pp. 61–79.

12. In 1969 the world price of rice was 2.88 times the price of wheat and that year China exported 712.5 thousand tons of rice, enabling it to import 2.052 million tons of wheat without using any foreign exchange. However, rice sales paid for less than two-thirds of its wheat imports that year. See Michael Allaby, *World Food Resources: Actual and Potential* (London: Applied Science

Publishers, 1977), p. 14. In 1974, a bad year for China, it spent $2 billion in foreign exchange to pay for grain. See *People's Republic of China; International Trade Handbook* (Washington, D.C.: Central Intelligence Agency, September 1974).

13. China has been importing sugar for a number of years. In 1976 it imported 1.5 million tons. China exported soybeans up until 1973; since then it has been an importer.

14. The term *important* here is based on weight, amount traded, and applications to engineering. These are also five of the six most common ferrous and nonferrous metals. For further discussion on this point, see Yuan-li Wu, *Raw Material Supply in a Multipolar World* (New York: Crane, Russak, 1973), p. 7.

15. Deleyne, *The Chinese Economy*, p. 155.

16. See *China: The Nonferrous Metals Industry in the 1970s* (Washington, D.C.: Central Intelligence Agency, 1978).

17. It is interesting to note in this connection that China has given extensive economic aid to both Zambia and Chile. This suggests that Peking is worried about a reliable supply of copper.

18. *Far Eastern Economic Review*, August 27, 1973. One recent report notes that China is also importing titanium, despite having domestic sources, due to the problems involved in processing. See Russell Spurr, "Peking: Beefing Up the Great Wall," *Far Eastern Economic Review*, June 18, 1976.

19. *The Financial Times*, January 27, 1976.

20. All of the above points are discussed in greater depth in Herman Kahn, William Brown, and Leon Martel, *The Next 200 Years: A Scenario for America and the World* (New York: William Morrow, 1975), chapter 4.

21. In 1974 China imported $400 million in fertilizers and raw materials, $250 million in nonferrous metals, and $200 million in pig iron, scrap iron, and ferrous metals. That same year it exported $150 million in "export metals" and $15 million each of salt, fluorspar, coal, talc, and manganese. See K. P. Wang, *Mineral Resources and Basic Industries in the People's Republic of China* (Boulder, Colo.: Westview Press, 1977), p. 202.

22. From 1970 to 1977 China imported metals—mainly aluminum, copper, nickel, and lead—worth $206 billion. During the same period its exports of metals amounted to only $645 million, or less than one-fourth of its imports. See *China: The Nonferrous Metals Industry in the 1970s*. This can be attributed in part to low investment in mining, poor transport facilities, and increased domestic use.

23. A. Doak Barnett, *Communist Economic Strategy: The Rise of Mainland China* (Washington, D.C.: National Planning Association, 1959), p. 22.

24. This figure is based on Peking's own estimates. A UNECAFE survey cited China's potential (excluding Sinkiang and Tibet) at 109,000,000 kilowatts, which compares with a pre-Communist estimate of 137,000,000 kilowatts for all of China. See Marcel Toussaint, "China's Energy Policies," in Curt Gasteyger, *The Western World and Energy* (Paris: The Atlantic Institute for International Affairs, 1974).

25. *China: Energy Balance Projections* (Washington, D.C.: Central Intelligence Agency, November 1975).

26. Ibid.

27. Ibid.

28. See John Ashton, "Development of Electric Energy Resources in Communist China," in *An Economic Profile of Mainland China, I* (Washington, D.C.: U.S. Government Printing Office, 1967), p. 299.

29. New China News Agency, December 26, 1977—quoted in *Facts on File*, December 31, 1977—cites a figure of 8 percent. Kyodo News Service (Tokyo), March 15, 1978, places the gains in Chinese oil sales in 1977 over 1976 at 6.8 percent.

30. Ibid. Also see Bruce J. Esposito, "China's Oil Prospects," *Asian Affairs*, July-August 1976. Both Thailand and the Philippines have experienced difficulties refining Chinese petroleum.

31. It is important to remember that, historically, natural resource cartels have not been successful for long periods of time. It also should be noted in this connection that because of the price increases after 1973, a large number of nations in all parts of the world have found oil and many more nations are now exporting oil than in the early 1970s.

32. *China: Energy Balance Projections* (Washington, D.C.: Central Intelligence Agency, November, 1975).

33. *Handbook of Economic Statistics, 1978*, p. 84.

34. See *China: Energy Balance Projections* for further details on this point.

35. *Survey of World Energy Resources*, (Washington, D.C.: Central Intelligence Agency, 1974).

CHAPTER 4

1. It is worth noting that economic sanctions or boycotts have not been applied successfully to any major power in the post-World War II period and that the only real effort to use such means was against China as a result of the Korean War. This endeavor tended to amplify in the minds of Chinese leaders the need for self-reliance, while it also tended to make China appear to be more economically self-sufficient than it really was.

2. There are about twenty major international cartels or producer cooperative organizations besides OPEC. China is not listed as a member of any of them. See Arthur S. Banks, ed., *Political Handbook of the World, 1976* (New York: McGraw-Hill, 1976), pp. 453–57. This source also cites a number of regional economic organizations, none of which includes China as a member.

3. During the 1960s China's foreign trade volume was somewhat less than that of Taiwan or Singapore. After 1972 China's trade increased markedly, but due to the fact that it built up a considerable foreign debt ($1 billion in 1974), it did not continue to grow as rapidly. In 1978 China's exports totaled $7.6 billion compared to Taiwan's $10.8 billion. See *Asia 1979 Yearbook*, p. 176 and 304.

4. *China: International Trade, 1976–77* (Washington, D.C.: National Foreign Assessment Center, 1977), p. 9.

5. See *China: Real Trends in Trade with Non-Communist Countries Since 1970* (Washington, D.C.: National Foreign Assessment Center, 1977), p. 3.

6. See Deleyne, *The Chinese Economy*, p. 162, for further details. The disparity is even greater in the case of the United States, which has been China's second or third major trading partner in recent years.

7. See John F. Copper, *China's Foreign Aid: An Instrument of Peking's Foreign Policy* (Lexington, Mass.: D. C. Heath, 1976) for further details.

8. Statistical information on this subject can be found in various issues of the *Monthly Bulletin of Statistics* (United Nations). It is worth noting here that over one-half of all foreign investment in recent years has come from the United States and very little from nations other than the United States and its allies.

9. Dwight H. Perkins, ed., *China's Modern Economy in Historical Perspective* (Stanford, Calif.: Stanford University Press, 1975), Introduction.

10. See Charles Hoffman, *The Chinese Worker* (Albany: State University of New York Press, 1975), pp. 3–4, for further details on this topic. Also see John Phillip Emerson, "Administrative and Technical Manpower in the People's Republic of China," *International Population Report Series P–95*, No. 72 (Washington, D.C.: U.S. Department of Commerce, 1973).

11. Richman, *Industrial Society in Communist China*, p. 137.

12. See Hoffman, *The Chinese Worker*, pp. 144–50, for further details on this point. The *New York Times*, August 3, 1975, reported that 10,000 troops had been sent to Hangchou to suppress labor violence there.

13. Because the United States has been and remains the world's most important exporter of capital and owing to its special relationship to Latin America, that area has received more foreign investment than Asia and Africa together. African and some Asian countries have become more favored in recent years, but Asia, in per capita terms, remains quite low—and China is at the bottom of the list.

14. Yuan-li Wu, *The Spatial Economy of Communist China: A Study on Industrial Location and Transportation* (New York: Praeger Publishers, 1967), chapter 3.

15. Several other sources put the total length of China's roads below the figures cited in Table 4–10. For example, see *Far Eastern Economic Review*, February 17, 1966, and *Japanese Economist*, July 1970.

16. See Audrey Donnithorne, "China's Cellular Economy: Some Trends Since the Cultural Revolution," *China Quarterly*, October-December 1972, for further details on this point.

17. Genevieve C. Dean, "Science, Technology and Development: China as a 'Case Study'," *China Quarterly*, July-September 1972.

18. See chapter 7 for further details on this point.

19. For a discussion of the disadvantages of size to China's economic development, see Alexander Eckstein, *China's Economic Development: The Interplay of Scarcity and Ideology* (Ann Arbor: University of Michigan Press, 1975), p. 12.

20. Refer to Table 4–2 for the source on these and following figures.

21. See the *Times* (London), December 4, 1972, for more detailed economic data, making possible a comparison of China's and India's economic development.

22. Much of the analysis that follows comes from Alfred H. Suack, Jr., and James D. Egan, "China's Iron and Steel Industry," in *China: A Reassessment of the Economy* (Washington, D.C.: U.S. Government Printing Office, 1975).

23. China's ranking as an economic power over the past two to three decades can be obtained from yearly issues of the *World Bank Atlas*. See for example *World Bank Atlas: Population, Per Capita Product, and Growth Rates* (Washington, D.C.: The World Bank, 1977), pp. 4−7.

24. *Handbook of Economic Statistics* (Washington, D.C.: Central Intelligence Agency, 1977), p. 28.

25. *Asia 1978 Yearbook*, (Hong Kong: Far Eastern Economic Review, Ltd., 1977), p. 166.

CHAPTER 5

1. Samuel B. Griffith II, *The Chinese People's Liberation Army* (New York: McGraw-Hill, 1963), pp. 270−72.

2. This conclusion is based upon the fact that China has been the only advancing nuclear power in recent years. France and the United Kingdom have stopped competing seriously in the arms race and, in any case, have tied their security to either the United States or the Western European community or both.

3. Frederic M. Kaplan, Julian M. Sobin and Stephen Andors, *Encyclopedia of China Today* (New York: Harper and Row, 1979), p. 95.

4. There are nearly 2 million Soviet troops on the Sino-Soviet border, plus 1,000 tanks, 2,000 military aircraft, and 20 missile sites, all aimed at China. See Harry Gerber, "Nuclear Weapons and Chinese Policy," *Adelphi Paper No. 99* (London: International Institute for Strategic Studies, 1976).

5. See William W. Whitson, *The Chinese High Command: A History of Communist Military Politics, 1927−71* (New York: Praeger, 1973), for an analysis of the various nonmilitary functions performed by the Chinese military as well as its influence in politics.

6. It should be noted that figures on China's defense spending are only estimates. For example *The Stratigic Survey*, which is the most quoted source and generally regarded as the most reliable, in its 1977 report put China's spending for defense at $10 to $17 billion. In 1978 it estimated it at $35 billion. The discrepancy is based on the use of different kinds of estimates.

7. The following give recent estimates on China's military budget: *The Strategic Survey, 1976−77* (based partly on U.S. Arms Control and Disarmament Agency estimates); Ruth L. Sivard, *World Military and Social Expenditures, 1978* (Leesburg, Virginia: WMSE Publications, 1978); Robert C. Sellers, ed., *Armed Forces of the World: A Reference Handbook* (New York: Praeger, 1977); *Far Eastern Economic Review*, May 7, 1976. The first estimates China's defense spending at $10−$17 billion. The second and third sources put it at $18 billion, and cites China as number three in defense spending although West Germany was ranked number three the previous year. The last source estimates China's defense budget at $10 billion, and ranks Iran above China. This source is older, but more recent reports by this magazine indicate China's defense spending has not increased significantly. In contrast, the U.S. Arms Control and Disarmament Agency in 1978 indicated a significant rise in defense spending in China, and put China in third place by a sub-

stantial margin. The estimate in Table 5–4 is based on 10 percent of China's GNP which is, therefore, an estimate on an estimate.

8. *The Military Balance, 1978–79* (London: The International Institute for Strategic Studies, 1978), p. 57.

9. Robert F. Dernberger, "Economic Consequences of Defense Expenditure Choices in China," in *China: A Reassessment of the Economy.*

10. See *The Military Balance, 1978–79,* for the figures on China's aircraft. A number of analysts argue that most of China's planes are badly in need of repair or are obsolescent. U.S. Secretary of Defense Harold Brown made statements to this effect to Congress in January 1979. For details see *Asian Wall Street Journal,* February 17, 1979. It is also worthy of note that China now imports a sizable number of its military aircraft from Japan, a nation not known for making sophisticated arms. These should not be designated combat planes. See Sellers, ed., *Armed Forces of the World,* p. 49.

11. Russell Spurr, "China's Defense: Men Against Machines," *Far Eastern Economic Review,* January 28, 1977. Another reason for the slowdown of production of this plane may be that the Chinese see it as already obsolete. Most defense analysts agree that it would not be competitive with present Soviet fighters, even in trying to defend China.

12. See Charles H. Murphy, "China's Evolving Nuclear Deterrent," *Bulletin of Atomic Scientists,* January 1972. The author compares this plane to the U.S. B–47, which was phased out after World War II.

13. The large number of naval craft in the Chinese navy is also explained by the fact that few private boats exist in China, in order to prevent people from leaving the country.

14. John E. Moore, ed., *Janes Fighting Ships, 1973–74* (London: Low, Marston, 1973), p. 103. Argentina, Brazil, and Spain also have helicopter aircraft carriers. As of early 1979, China's only nuclear submarine was still under construction.

15. See *The Military Balance, 1978–79.*

16. Statistics on the strength of the Chinese army in terms of type of divisions, weapons, etc. can be found in *Handbook on the Chinese Armed Forces* (Washington, D.C.: Defense Intelligence Agency, July 1976), chapter 1.

17. Whitson, *The Chinese High Command,* p. 555.

18. A number of experts on the Chinese military note problems of morale and internal conflict. See the following: Chester Cheng, *The Politics of the Red Chinese Army* (Stanford, Calif.: Hoover Institution Press, 1966); Ellis Joffee, "The Chinese Army After the Cultural Revolution: The Effects of Intervention," *China Quarterly,* July-September 1973, and ibid.

19. *The Military Balance, 1976–77.* This source notes that the United States will have over 10,000 nuclear warheads for missiles by 1980, and that the Soviet Union will reach that number shortly thereafter. Since this does not include warheads for bombers, it is assumed that both are well past the 10,000 mark now.

20. In 1976, 19 nations had nuclear reactors in use for generating power—not including China. By 1984 there are predicted to be 31 nations. See *World Armaments and Disarmament SIPRI Yearbook* (Stockholm: Stockholm International Peace Research Institute, 1977).

21. China also lacks the capability for military attacks from space possessed by the United States, the Soviet Union, the United Kingdom, and France or for building space-based weapons systems. See Sellers, ed., *Armed Forces of the World*, p. 264.

22. See C. G. Jacobson, "Strategic Considerations Affecting Soviet Policy Toward China and Japan," *Orbis*, Winter 1974. This author makes an impressive argument that the Soviet Union is not vulnerable to a Chinese nuclear attack.

23. This opinion is reflected in a number of publications of the London Institute for Strategic Studies.

24. See Chalmers Johnson, *Autopsy of People's War* (Berkeley: University of California Press, 1974) for a detailed account of this argument.

25. In 1976, China was a major supplier of arms to only three Third World nations, two of which were also receiving large quantities of military supplies from the United States and other Western countries. See *World Armaments and Disarmaments SIPRI Yearbook, 1977*.

26. Peter G. Mueller and Douglas A. Rose, *China and Japan—Emerging Global Powers* (New York: Praeger, 1975), p. 105.

27. Most students of China's foreign policy do not regard China as having an aggressive foreign policy or having clearly started the wars in which it has been involved since 1949. See, for example, Allen S. Whiting, *China Crosses the Yalu: The Decision to Enter the Korean War* (New York: Macmillan, 1960), and his "The Use of Force in Foreign Policy by the People's Republic of China," the *Annals*, July 1972; Nevil Maxwell, *India's China War* (New York: Anchor Books, 1972); and James C. Hsiung, *Law and Policy in China's Foreign Relations: A Study of Attitudes and Practices* (New York: Columbia University Press, 1972).

28. It should be noted in this regard that the statements made by Mao to the effect that China can "lose three hundred million people in a nuclear war and still defeat the imperialists" is a second-hand statement. Furthermore, it may be interpreted as a kind of positive thinking. After all, Mao could not have been expected to say that China was defenseless and vulnerable to threats and intimidation by the United States and other powers. Finally, China's so-called reckless statements have not been followed by actions. China has not provided any other country with atomic weapons or threatened any other country with them, in marked contrast to the behavior of the United States and the Soviet Union. Instead, China has made a no-first-use pledge which seems to be sincere.

29. Sellers lists eight nations with "impending" capabilities and twenty more nations with "future" capabilities. He cites both India and Israel as present nuclear powers. See Sellers, ed., *Armed Forces of the World*, p. 263.

CHAPTER 6

1. Derek J. Waller, *The Government Politics of Communist China* (London: Hutchinson University Library, 1970), pp. 34–35. The author also notes that the Communist party in China is smaller than in any other Communist nation in terms of percent of population.

2. For a discussion of the three primary centers of political power—party, government, and military—see A. Doak Barnett, *Uncertain Passage: China's Transition to the Post-Mao Era* (Washington, D.C.: The Brookings Institution, 1974), chapter 1.

3. For an excellent analysis of the problem of bureaucratism in China, see A. Doak Barnett, *Cadres, Bureaucracy and Political Power in Communist China* (New York: Columbia University Press, 1967).

4. See Starr, *Ideology and Culture*, p. 155; and Jurgen Domes, "Transition Toward a New Political System in China: The Role of the Party and the Army," in Ian Wilson, ed., *China and the World Community* (Sydney: Angus & Robertson, 1973). The former makes this argument on the basis of the need for revolutionary changes in China; the latter contends that China has not yet found a satisfactory political system.

5. David Bonavia, "Six of the Best for Chairman Hua," *Far Eastern Economic Review*, May 27, 1977.

6. For a discussion of these and various other changes in the nature of the Chinese leadership, see Robert A. Scalapino, ed., *Elites in the People's Republic of China* (Seattle: University of Washington Press, 1972).

7. See Andrew J. Nathan, "A Factional Model for Chinese Communist Party Politics," *China Quarterly*, January-March, 1973.

8. Barnett, *Uncertain Passage*, p. 608.

9. See Victor C. Falkenheim, "Provincial Leadership in Fukien," in Scalapino, ed., *Elites in the People's Republic of China*, p. 200.

10. Jurgen Domes, *The Internal Politics of China, 1949–1972* (New York: Praeger, 1973), p. 217.

11. James N. Townsend, *Politics in China*, (New York: Little, Brown, 1974), pp. 78 and 311–15.

12. See Barnett, *Uncertain Passage*, chapter 1.

13. See Jack Gray, ed., *China's Search for Political Form* (London: Oxford University Press, 1969), for a detailed account of the changes in the Chinese political system.

14. According to a number of writers, China lacks the prerequisites to be regarded as possessing a centralized political system. See, for example, Victor C. Falkenheim, "Provincial Leadership in Fukien," in Scalapino, ed., *Elites in the People's Republic of China*, pp. 200–201. James Townsend makes a similar point in discussing the political modernization process in China. See Townsend, *Politics in China*, pp. 186–87.

15. Marion Levy suggests that centralized political systems require a highly integrated society and a modern communications and logistics network. See Marion J. Levy, Jr., *Modernization and the Structure of Society: A Setting for International Affairs* (Princeton: Princeton University Press, 1966), p. 17. Scholars who have defined the totalitarian model cite effective mass communications as a requirement. See, for example, Friedrich and Brzezinski, *Totalitarian Dictatorship and Autocracy*.

16. *Encyclopedia Britannica*, 1975.

17. Ibid.

18. Townsend, *Politics in China*, pp. 135–36 and 275–76.

19. Barnett, *Uncertain Passage*, pp. 101–02.

20. Charles L. Taylor and Michael C. Hudson, *World Handbook of Political and Social Indicators*, (New Haven: Yale University Press, 1972), p. 110.

21. Chadwick F. Alger and Steven J. Brams, "Patterns of Representation in National Capitals and Intergovernmental Organizations," *World Politics*, July 1967.

22. See Melvin Gurtov, "The Foreign Ministry and Foreign Affairs During the Cultural Revolution," *China Quarterly*, October-December, 1969.

23. It is worthwhile noting, in this connection, that the travel experiences and contacts with foreign countries are decreasing as the leadership ages and more younger people assume positions of importance. See Donald W. Klein, "The Next Generation of Chinese Communist Leaders," in Roderick Mac-Farquhar, ed., *China Under Mao: Politics Takes Command* (Cambridge: Massachusetts Institute of Technology Press, 1966).

24. See Swadesh Rana, "China's Low Profile at the U.N.," *China Report*, May-June, 1973. It also should be noted that China is not a member of any of the following major international organizations: General Agreement on Trade and Tariffs, International Atomic Energy Commission, International Bank for Reconstruction and Development, International Development Association, International Finance Corporation, International Monetary Fund, and World Intellectual Property Organization. All of these have a majority of nations of the world as members.

25. See Samuel S. Kim, "China and World Order," *Alternatives*, May 1978.

26. *World Military Expenditures and Arms Transfers, 1966–75* (Washington, D.C.: U.S. Arms Control and Disarmament Agency, December 1976).

27. See Copper, *China's Foreign Aid*, chapter 6.

28. Barnett, *Uncertain Passage*, p. 187.

29. For an assessment of U.S. violations of China's territorial integrity and China's reaction, see *China: Inside the People's Republic* (New York: Bantam Books, 1972), pp. 324–26.

30. Peking has frequently made statements to the effect that the atomic bomb is a paper tiger. Mao has reportedly stated that China could lose up to 300 million people in an atomic war and "still defeat the imperialists." It should be kept in mind, however, that some of the most reckless statements supposedly made by Mao were reported first by Indian leaders and that Mao's statements regarding the atomic bomb not being a decisive weapon were made for domestic consumption and may represent nothing more than an effort at positive thinking. He certainly could not have been expected to tell the people of China that their enemies had weapons that could obliterate China and Peking could do nothing about it. Chinese pronouncements also should be contrasted to statements concerning peaceful intentions, no-first-use, and so forth. In this connection, see "Statement of the Government of the People's Republic of China," *Peking Review*, October 16, 1964.

31. In contrast, China has been threatened with nuclear weapons on at least four occasions. See P. R. Chari, "China's Nuclear Posture: An Evaluation," *Asian Survey*, August 1978.

CHAPTER 7

1. Immanuel C. Y. Hsu, "The Reorganization of Higher Education in Communist China, 1949–61," in Roderick MacFarquhar, ed., *China Under Mao: Politics Takes Command.*

2. John M. H. Lindbeck, "The Organization and Development of Science," in ibid.

3. See R. F. Price, *Education in Communist China* (New York: Praeger, 1970), p. 202, for figures on illiteracy in China prior to 1949. According to Chinese officials, the illiteracy rate was reduced to 20 to 30 percent by 1959 (cited in Price, p. 196). In 1964 an official statement from Peking cited 20 percent as the number of illiterate and semiliterate in China *(People's Daily,* January 26, 1964). However, China's definition of literacy is not as rigid as Western or international standards.

4. Thomas P. Bernstein, "Implications of Educational Policy for the Economic and Social Future of the PRC," (paper presented at the Sino-American Conference on China at Georgetown University in Washington, D.C., in June 1977). These data also appear in the author's book entitled *Up to the Mountains and Down to the Villages: The Transfer of Youth from Urban to Rural China* (New Haven: Yale University Press, 1977).

5. Hsu, "The Reorganization of Higher Education in Communist China, 1949–61."

6. The *World* (Hong Kong) July 1973.

7. Wilson, *Anatomy of China,* p. 155.

8. Hans Heyman, Jr., "Self-Reliance Revisited: China's Technological Dilemma," *Stanford Journal of International Studies,* Spring 1975.

9. The evidence for this view is the fact that nothing has been done in this direction in recent years, and whenever the subject is brought up it is quickly shelved.

10. For further details on this point, see Richard P. Suttmeier, *Research and Revolution: Science Policy and Societal Change in China* (Lexington, Mass.: D.C. Heath, 1974), especially p. 47.

11. *Washington Post,* August 8, 1973.

12. Bruce J. Esposito, "The Cultural Revolution and China's Scientific Establishment," *Current Scene,* August 1974.

13. Bernstein, "Implications of Educational Policy for the Economic and Social Future of the PRC."

14. For further details on the influence of the Cultural Revolution on China's education and science, see A. Doak Barnett, "More Thoughts Out of China: There are Warts There Too," *New York Times Magazine,* April 8, 1973.

15. It should be noted in this regard that in expenditures on education China ranks just above the world's average, even though it has the world's largest population. On a per capita basis, China spends $4.00 per year per person, while the world's average is $24.55. The source for this information is the same as for Table 7–9.

16. *Science Indicators* (Washington, D.C.: U.S. National Science Board, 1975).

17. *Science Citation Index* (Philadelphia: Institute of Scientific Information, 1974).

18. Ibid.

19. For further details on this point, see Richard P. Suttmeier, "Science Policy Shifts, Organizational Change and China's Development," *China Quarterly*, June 1975.

20. Joseph Anderson Shih, "Science and Technology in China," *Asian Survey*, August 1972.

21. For further details on this point, see Rensselaer W. Lee III, "The Politics of Technology in Communist China," in Chalmers Johnson, ed., *Ideology and Politics in Contemporary China* (Seattle: University of Washington Press, 1973), p. 325.

22. Further details can be found in Dean, "Science, Technology and Development: China as a Case Study."

23. Hans Heyman, Jr., "Acquisition and Diffusion of Technology in China," in *China: A Reassessment of the Economy*, pp. 670–729.

CHAPTER 8

1. John H. Hertz, "The Rise and Demise of the Territorial State," *World Politics* 9 (1957).

2. See Kahn, et al. *The Next 200 Years*, chapter 4.
chapter 4.

3. See Richard A. Falk, *A Study of Future Worlds* (New York: The Free Press, 1975), p. 91.

4. See Victor Basiuk, *Technology, World Politics and American Policy* (New York: Columbia University Press, 1977), p. 5, and Ferris, *The Power Capabilities of Nation-States*, p. 37.

5. See P. R. Chari, "China's Nuclear Posture: An Education," *Asian Survey*, August 1978.

6. This has led a number of authors to use new terms to describe an international system in which elements of bipolarity remain. One author uses the term *bipolycentrism*; another *bimultipolarity*. See John Spanier, *Games Nations Play: Analyzing International Politics* (New York: Praeger, 1975), chapter 4, and Richard N. Rosecrance, "Bipolarity, Multipolarity and the Future," *Journal of Conflict Resolution*, No. 10 (1966).

7. See Klaus Knorr, *On the Uses of Military Power in the Nuclear Age* (Princeton: Princeton University Press, 1966).

8. Alastair Buchan, *Power and Equilibrium in the 1970s* (New York: Praeger, 1973), pp. 13–30.

9. Rosecrance, "Bipolarity, Multipolarity and the Future."

10. Karl Deutsch and J. David Singer, "Multipolar Power Systems and International Stability," *World Politics*, April 1964.

11. Cecil V. Crabb, Jr., *Nations in a Multipolar World* (New York: Harper & Row, 1968).

12. See Thomas C. Schelling, "The Role of Deterrence in Total Disarmament," *Foreign Affairs*, April 1962.

13. Paul Seabury, *The Rise and Decline of the Cold War* (New York: Basic Books, 1967), p. 59.

14. This point is argued both pro and con by George Liska, *Nations in Alliance* (Baltimore, Md.: Johns Hopkins University Press, 1962).

15. See Morgenthau, *Politics Among Nations*, chapter 10.

Bibliography

Aidie, W. A. C. *Chinese Strategic Thinking under Mao Tse-tung.* Canberra: Australian National University Press, 1972.

Andors, Stephen. *China's Industrial Revolution: Politics, Planning and Management, 1949 to the Present.* New York: Pantheon, 1977.

Asia 1979 Yearbook. Hong Kong: Far Eastern Economic Review, 1978.

Banister, Judith, "International Effects of China's Population Situation," in *China's Changing Role in the World Economy.* Edited by Bryant G. Garth. New York: Praeger, 1975.

Barendsen, Robert. *The Educational Revolution in China.* Washington, D.C.: U.S. Government Printing Office, 1973.

Barnett, A. Doak. *Cadres, Bureaucracy and Political Power in Communist China.* New York: Columbia University Press, 1967.

————. *Uncertain Passage: China's Transition to the Post-Mao Era.* Washington, D.C.: Brookings Institution Press, 1974.

Bernstein, Thomas P. *Up the Mountains and Down to the Villages: The Transfer of Youth from Urban to Rural China.* New Haven: Yale University Press, 1977.

Buchanan, Keith. *The Transformation of the Chinese Earth.* New York: Praeger, 1970.

Chen, Huan-i. "Agricultural Modernization and Modernization in China," *Current History,* September 1976.

Chen, Nai-ruenn, ed. *Chinese Economic Statistics: A Handbook for Mainland China.* Chicago: Aldine, 1967.

Chen, Theodore H. E. "The Maoist Model of Education: Theory and Practice," *Asian Survey,* September-October 1976.

Cheng, Chester J., ed. *The Politics of the Chinese Red Army.* Stanford, Calif.: Hoover Institution Press, 1966.

Cheng, Chu-yuan. *China's Petroleum Industry: Output, Growth and Export Potential.* New York: Praeger, 1976.

China: A Reassessment of the Economy. Washington, D.C.: U.S. Government Printing Office, 1975.

China: Energy Balance Projections. Washington, D.C.: Central Intelligence Agency, 1975.

China: In Pursuit of Economic Modernization. Washington, D.C.: Central Intelligence Agency, 1978.

China: International Trade, 1977-78. Washington, D.C.: Central Intelligence Agency, 1978.

China: Oil Production Prospects. Washington, D.C.: Central Intelligence Agency, 1977.

China: The Coal Industry. Washington, D.C.: Central Intelligence Agency, 1976.

China: The Nonferrous Metals Industry in the 1970s. Washington, D.C.: Central Intelligence Agency, 1978.

China and the Chinese: A Compendium of Papers. Washington, D.C.: U.S. Government Printing Office, 1976.

Chinese Economy Post-Mao. Washington, D.C.: U. S. Government Printing Office, 1978.

Clough, Ralph N., et al. *The United States, China and Arms Control.* Washington, D.C.: Brookings Institution Press, 1975.

Copper, John F. *China's Foreign Aid.* Lexington, Mass.: D. C. Heath, 1976.

Dean, Genevieve C. "Science, Technology and Development: China as a Case Study," *China Quarterly.* July-September 1972.

Dean, Genevieve, and François Godement, eds. *Science and Technology in the People's Republic of China.* Washington, D.C.: OECD Publications, 1977.

Deleyne, Jan. *The Chinese Economy.* New York: Harper and Row, 1974.

Domes, Jurgen, *China after the Cultural Revolution.* Berkeley: University of California Press, 1977.

Donnithorne, Audrey. *China's Economic System.* New York: Praeger, 1967.

————. "China's Cellular Economy: Some Trends since the Cultural Revolution," *China Quarterly,* October-December 1972.

Eckstein, Alexander. *China's Economic Development: The Interplay of Scarcity and Ideology.* Ann Arbor: University of Michigan Press, 1975.

————. *China's Economic Revolution.* Cambridge: Cambridge University Press, 1977.

Esposito, Bruce J. "The Cultural Revolution and China's Scientific Establishment," *Current Scene,* August 1974.

————. "China's Oil Prospects," *Asian Affairs,* July-August, 1976.

Fingar, Thomas. *China's Energy Policies and Resource Development.* Stanford, Calif.: U.S. China Relations Program, 1976.

Food and Agricultural Yearbook. New York: United Nations, 1976.

Freeberne, Michael. "Physical and Social Geography," in *The Far East and Australia: 1977–78.* London: Europa, 1977.

Gamberg, Ruth. *Red and Expert: Education in the People's Republic of China.* New York: Schocken, 1977.

George, Alexander L. *The Chinese Communist Army in Action.* New York: Columbia University Press, 1967.

Gerber, Harry. "Nuclear Weapons and Chinese Policy," Adelphia Paper no. 99. London: International Institute of Strategic Studies, 1976.

Ghosh, S. K., and Sreedhar, eds. *China's Nuclear and Political Strategy.* New Delhi: Young Asian Publications, 1975.

Gittings, John. *The Role of the Chinese Army.* London: Oxford University Press, 1967.

Gray, Jack, ed. *China's Search for Political Form*. London: Oxford University Press, 1969.

Griffith, Samuel B., II. *The Chinese People's Liberation Army*. New York: McGraw-Hill, 1963.

Gurtov, Melvin. "The Foreign Ministry and Foreign Affairs during the Cultural Revolution," *China Quarterly*, October-December 1969.

Handbook on the Chinese Armed Forces. Washington, D.C.: U.S. Defense Intelligence Agency, 1976.

Handbook of Economic Statistics: 1978. Washington, D.C.: Central Intelligence Agency, 1978.

Heyman, Hans, Jr. "Self-Reliance Revisited: China's Technological Dilemma," *Stanford Journal of International Studies*, Spring 1975.

Hinton, Harold C. *Communist China in World Politics*. Boston: Houghton Mifflin, 1964.

————. *The Sino-Soviet Confrontation: Implications for the Future*. New York: Crane, Russak, 1976.

Hoffman, Charles. *The Chinese Worker*. Albany: State University of New York Press, 1975.

Hsiao, Gene T. *The Foreign Trade of China: Policy, Law and Practice*. Berkeley: University of California Press, 1977.

Hsieh, Alice. *Communist China's Strategy in the Nuclear Era*. Englewood Cliffs, N.J.: Prentice-Hall, 1962.

Hsiung, James Chieh. *Law and Policy in China's Foreign Relations: A Study of Attitudes and Practices*. New York: Columbia University Press, 1972.

Joffe, Ellis. *Party and Army: Professionalism and Political Control in the Chinese Officers Corps, 1949–1964*. Cambridge: Harvard University Press, 1965.

Johnson, Chalmers. *Autopsy on People's War*. Berkeley: University of California Press, 1974.

Kaplan, Frederick, et al. *Encyclopedia of China Today*. Fairlawn, N.J.: Eurasia, 1979.

Kim, Samuel S. *China, the United Nations and World Order*. Princeton: Princeton University Press, 1979.

Lindbeck, John M., ed. *China: Management of a Revolutionary Society*. Seattle: University of Washington Press, 1971.

Ling, H. C. *Petroleum Industry of the People's Republic of China*. Stanford, Calif.: Hoover Institution Press, 1975.

MacFarquhar, Roderick, ed. *China under Mao: Politics Takes Command*. Cambridge: MIT Press, 1966.

The Military Balance, 1978–79. London: International Institute for Strategic Studies, 1978.

Mineral Review Yearbook of the Mineral Industry of Mainland China. Pittsburgh: U.S. Department of Interior, 1975.

Mueller, Peter G., and Douglas A. Rose. *China and Japan: Emerging Global Powers*. New York: Praeger, 1975.

Nathan, Andrew J. "A Factional Model for Chinese Communist Party Politics," *China Quarterly*, January-March 1973.

North, Robert C. *The Foreign Relations of China*. North Scituate, Mass.: Duxbury, 1978.

Ojha, Ishwer. *China's Foreign Relations in an Age of Transition: The Diplomacy of Cultural Despair*. Boston: Beacon, 1969.

Orleans, Leo. *Every Fifth Child: The Population of China*. Stanford: Stanford University Press, 1972.

———. *China's Birth Rate, Death Rate, and Population Growth: Another Perspective*. Washington, D.C.: U.S. Government Printing Office, 1977.

Perkins, Dwight H., ed. *China's Modern Economy in Historical Perspective*. Stanford: Stanford University Press, 1975.

Prybyla, Jan S. "The Asian Dilemma: Reordering National Priorities," *Current History*, June 1975.

———. *The Chinese Economy: Problems and Prospects*. Columbia: University of South Carolina Press, 1978.

Richman, Barry M. *Industrial Society in Communist China*. New York: Praeger, 1969.

Ridley, Charles P. *China's Scientific Policies: Implications for International Cooperation*. Washington, D.C.: American Enterprise Institute, 1976.

Rohn, Peter H. *Treaty Profiles*. Santa Barbara: Clio, 1976.

Scalapino, Robert A., ed. *Elites in the People's Republic of China*. Seattle: University of Washington Press, 1972.

Sellers, Robert C., ed. *Armed Forces of the World: A Reference Handbook*. New York: Praeger, 1977.

Shabed, Theodore. *China's Changing Map*. New York: Praeger, 1956.

Shih, Joseph Anderson. "Science and Technology in China," *Asian Survey*, August 1972.

Smil, Vaclav. *Energy in China: Achievements and Prospects*. New York: Praeger, 1976.

———. "Intermediate Energy Technology in China," *Bulletin of Atomic Scientists*, February 1977.

Spurr, Russell. "Peking: Beefing Up the Great Wall," *Far Eastern Economic Review*, June 18, 1976.

———. "China's Defense: Men against Machines," *Far Eastern Economic Review*, January 28, 1977.

The Strategic Survey: 1977. London: International Institute for Strategic Studies, 1978.

Survey of Energy Resources. Washington, D.C.: Central Intelligence Agency, 1974.

Suttmeier, Richard P. "Science Policy Shifts, Organizational Change and China's Development," *China Quarterly*, June 1975.

Taylor, Charles, and Michael C. Hudson. *World Handbook of Political and Social Indicators*. New Haven: Yale University Press, 1972.

Tien, H. Yuan. *China's Population Struggle: Demographic Decisions of the PRC: 1949–65*. Columbus: Ohio State University Press, 1973.

Townsend, James N. *Politics in China.* New York: Little, Brown, 1974.

Tsou, Tang, ed. *China in Crisis.* Chicago: University of Chicago Press, 1968.

United Nations Statistical Yearbook: 1977. New York: United Nations, 1978.

Waller, Derek J. *The Government and Politics of Communist China.* London: Hutchinson University Library, 1970.

Wang, K. P. *Mineral Resources and Basic Industries in the People's Republic of China.* Boulder: Westview, 1977.

Whiting, Allen S. *China Crosses the Yalu: The Decision to Enter the Korean War.* New York: Macmillan, 1960.

———. "The Use of Force in Foreign Policy by the People's Republic of China," *The Annals,* July 1972.

Whitson, William W. *The Chinese High Command: A History of Communist Military Politics, 1927–71.* New York: Praeger, 1973.

Whitson, William W., ed. *Doing Business with China: American Trade Opportunities in the 1970s.* New York: Praeger, 1974.

Who's Who in the United Nations and Related Agencies. New York: United Nations, 1975.

Wilson, Ian, ed. *China and the World Community.* Sydney: Angus and Robertson, 1973.

World Armaments and Disarmament SIPRI Yearbook. Stockholm: Stockholm International Peace Research Institute, 1977.

World Statistics in Brief. New York: United Nations, 1976.

Wu, Yuan-li. *The Spacial Economy of Communist China: A Study on Industrial Location and Transportation.* New York: Praeger, 1967.

———. *China: A Handbook.* New York: Praeger, 1973.

Index

Page numbers for information specifically found in tables are in italics.